John W. Ewing

Goodly Fellowship

The International Council and the Secretary General of the World Evangelical Alliance have decided that the whole year following the 175th birthday of the WEA Alliance will be a jubilee year with stories from the 143 national evangelical alliances to stir up thanks and prayer to God.

World of Theology Series

**Published by the Theological Commission
of the World Evangelical Alliance**

Volume 23

John W. Ewing

Goodly Fellowship
A Centenary Tribute to the Life and Work of the World's Evangelical Alliance 1846–1946

Jubilee Reprint of the 1946 Edition

WIPF & STOCK · Eugene, Oregon

Wipf and Stock Publishers
199 W 8th Ave, Suite 3
Eugene, OR 97401

Goodly Fellowship
A Centenary Tribute to the Life and Work of the World's Evangelical Alliance 1846-1946: Jubilee Reprint of the 1946 Edition
By Ewing, John W.
Copyright © 2022 Verlag für Kultur und Wissenschaft Culture and Science Publ.
All rights reserved.
Softcover ISBN-13: 978-1-6667-4523-8
Hardcover ISBN-13: 978-1-6667-4524-5
Publication date 4/18/2022
Previously published by Verlag für Kultur und Wissenschaft Culture and Science Publ., 2022

Four Early Leaders of the Alliance.
Above, The Hon. Baptist W. Noel, Dr. James Hamilton.
Below, Dr. Edward Steane, Hon. W. S. Dodge (U.S.A.).

SIR CULLING EARDLEY EARDLEY BART. F.R.G.S. &c.

Face page 5

CONTENTS

LIST OF ILLUSTRATIONS 6
INTRODUCTORY NOTE, JANUARY 2022 7
PRESS RELEASE 175 YEARS OF W.E.A. 8
PREFACE 10

I. THE WORLD IN 1846 11
II. BIRTH OF THE ALLIANCE 13
III. THE ALLIANCE BRANCHING OUT 22
IV. MILESTONES OF ADVANCE 25
V. THE ALLIANCE AND PRAYER 36
VI. THE PROCLAMATION OF THE GOSPEL 41
VII. PROTESTANT WITNESS 49
VIII. RELIGIOUS LIBERTY AND SUCCOUR OF THE PERSECUTED 58
IX. THE ALLIANCE AND THE LORD'S DAY 80
X. DEFENCE OF THE FAITH 85
XI. CARE FOR DEPRESSED RACES 93
XII. THE ALLIANCE AND MISSIONS 98
XIII. CELEBRATIONS MARKING HISTORY, 1896–1946 107
XIV. "EVANGELICAL CHRISTENDOM" 117
XV. INCORPORATION OF ALLIANCE (BRITISH ORGANISATION) 129
XVI. THE HEADQUARTERS 130
XVII. OFFICIALS AT THE CENTRE 132
XVIII. ALLIANCE LEADERS AND HELPERS 136
XIX. WHAT OF THE FUTURE? 146
EPILOGUE 151
INDEX 153

LIST OF ILLUSTRATIONS

Four Early Leaders of the Alliance	*Facing p. 4*
Sir Culling Eardley Eardley, Bart., F.R.G.S.	*Facing p. 5*
The New York (U.S.A.) Conference, 1873	*Facing p. 32*
The Amsterdam Conference of the Alliance, 1867	*Facing p. 33*
400th Anniversary of the Augsburg Confession	*Between pp. 48-49*
International Protestant League Conference Group	*Between pp. 48-49*
British Empire Exhibition, 1925-26	*Between pp. 48-49*
Back view of the Bungalow	*Between pp. 48-49*
Prayer Book Revision. The Royal Albert Hall Meeting arranged by the Alliance, 1925	*Between pp. 48-49*
Part of Letter of Thanks sent by the Council of the Alliance to the Shah of Persia for granting religious liberty	*Between pp. 72-73*
Design on Silk Handkerchief prepared to commemorate the founding of the Alliance in London, 1846	*Between pp. 72-73*
Religious Liberty in Turkey. Letter of Appeal from the Alliance to the Sultan	*Between pp. 72-73*
Eleventh International Conference, London, 1907	*Facing p. 96*
80th Anniversary Celebrations, 1927	*Facing p. 97*
H.R.H. The Duke of Kent addressing the great meeting in the Royal Albert Hall in celebration of the Silver Jubilee of King George V's Accession to the Throne	*Facing p. 128*
Waldensian Church House at Torre Pellice (Italy)	*Facing p. 129*
Moderator and Members of Synod in procession to open proceedings	*Facing p. 129*

INTRODUCTORY NOTE, JANUARY 2022

175TH ANNIVERSARY OF THE FOUNDING OF THE W.E.A.

AUGUST 26, 2021, marks the 175th anniversary of the founding of the "World's Evangelical Alliance". On August 1846 in central London 4,000 people attended that momentous event, with 15,000 unable to gain admittance. The past 175 years have proved to be momentous in many ways. Dr J. W. Ewing's history of the first hundred years gives a vivid account of the enthusiasm and innovation of our predecessors, which was reflected in society generally, with the introduction of railways, steam powered ships and underwater telephone cables, transforming the world into a global village. For evangelical Christians it meant taking the good news of the Gospel to the ends of the Earth. In the same era the Catholic church was seeking to reinforce its dominance and adding new doctrines to its list of non-biblical beliefs, such as the Immaculate Conception that the First Vatican Council adopted as dogma in 1870.

My first encounter with the "World's Evangelical Alliance" came somewhat as a surprise when I made my first visit to the offices of the UK Evangelical Alliance in 30 Bedford Square, London. I was acquainted with the "World Evangelical Fellowship" and had known that the "World's Evangelical Alliance" had existed until the late 1940's, after which the "World Evangelical Fellowship" had been formed in the Netherlands in 1951. But before my eyes as I approached the front door of 30 Bedford Square was a doormat which read "World's Evangelical Alliance". I was fascinated to find out the connection between the WEA and the WEF. Below, at the end of Dr Ewing's history, I add some words of my own to explain the connection between the WEA of 1846 and the WEF, which was renamed "World Evangelical Alliance" in 2008.

I hope you are as fascinated as I was when I read Dr Ewing's account of our illustrious predecessors in the pages which follow. Today we stand on the shoulders of giants as we seek to further the Kingdom of God in our own very different generation.

JOHN LANGLOIS, WEA International Council Member
January 2022

PRESS RELEASE 175 YEARS OF W.E.A.

175 years ago today, some 800 evangelical leaders from eleven countries representing fifty-two Christian denominations resolved to establish the WEA. They described it as a new thing in Church history – a definite organization for the expression of unity amongst Christian individuals belonging to different churches. Building on the momentum of the Great Awakenings and with a desire to respond to some of the grave social issues in society, they came together from all backgrounds of evangelicalism at that time.

The WEA continues to be a testimony for the fact that amid the incredible diversity, evangelicals be united together as one. In 1846, the churches came from the whole spectrum of the Protestant faith: from Reformation times, such as Anglicans, Lutherans, Reformed and Anabaptists; from the following centuries, such as Baptists, Methodists and later the Salvation Army; and today it also includes many newer churches formed in the 20th century, such as Pentecostals, Charismatics and Independents. Also considering the fact that each national Evangelical Alliance and each regional Alliance has its own unique history, and that evangelicals come from hundreds of ethnic groups and speak around 1,000 languages, the WEA is as colorful as never before. And this is something we would like to recognize through this Jubilee.

From the beginning, the WEA was established to foster unity with a purpose and mission. It has promoted the annual week of prayer for unity that is still observed in several countries to this day; it has encouraged the sharing of the Gospel of Jesus Christ; it has advocated for religious freedom for people of all faith – which made the WEA the first global faith body to do so; and it has responded to social issues, such as slavery and child labor.

Since then, the WEA has grown to a truly global organization with national Evangelical Alliances established in 143 countries on all continents. The WEA has now become the second largest world Church body that speaks as a representative voice on behalf of evangelicals at the United Nations, to governments and media, contributing an evangelical perspective on issues that are relevant to the Church globally. And it remains engaged in many of the same areas, including prayer, mission and a range of human rights and social justice issues, all based on the foundation in Scripture.

As a global network that has its roots in the local churches in the neighborhoods, we continue to hold on to the central role of Jesus Christ as our personal savior, the Bible as our supreme constitution and the goal to transform the world by preaching and practicing the "evangel", the gospel.

The year-long anniversary commemoration will start off in the coming week with daily social media postings featuring prayer topics from each region on the theme of unity.

Prayer has always been foundational to the WEA, so we want to begin the Jubilee by recognizing the diversity of the global body of Christ and the unique opportunities and challenges they face. We are very conscious that amid the ongoing pandemic and various other natural or man-made disasters, there is a great need for prayer today. So we invite you to join us as we commemorate 175 years and as we continue to put every effort into fulfilling Jesus' prayer that all of us may be one, so that the world may believe. (John 17:21-23)

Bishop Dr THOMAS SCHIRRMACHER,
Secretary General of the WEA

August 20, 2021

PREFACE

I ACCOUNT it a privilege to have been asked to prepare this centenary volume of the World's Evangelical Alliance. As I have proceeded with the necessary study I have been impressed with the magnitude of the work achieved during the hundred years, and have been touched by the glowing spirit of faith and love breathed by the founders and many of those who followed them. I feel it appropriate that the title of the book recalls the Te Deum, for the centenary of the Alliance is an event which calls forth rejoicing and praise. My authorities for the history have been the following: *The Report of the Proceedings of the Inaugural Conference; The Evangelical Alliance, its Origin and Development,* by J. W. Massie; *The Jubilee of the Evangelical Alliance,* edited by A. J. Arnold; *Manuel Matamoros and His Fellow-Prisoners in Spain*, by W. Greene; *Narrative of the European Deputation to Madrid in May, 1863*, by Edward Steane; and *Evangelical Christendom*, the magazine devoted to the work and fellowship of the Alliance. This publication, running from 1847 onward, is a rich storehouse of information on the subject. I have to thank Mr. H. M. Gooch, the General Secretary of the Alliance, for many helpful suggestions.

J. W. EWING.

Dr. J. W. Ewing, the Author of this volume, is a Vice-President of the World's Evangelical Alliance, and a past President of the National Council of the Evangelical Free Churches. His activities and work have gone far beyond denominational limitations, embracing all major Evangelical and Protestant interests in this country and overseas. Dr. Ewing has had access to sources of information enabling him to present a highly interesting as well as informative review of the witness and work of the Alliance during the century. But this volume is not only a record; it is a call to spiritual advance in fulfilment of a great destiny.

CHAPTER I

THE WORLD IN 1846

IN 1846 Queen Victoria, in the charm of her youth, had been on the throne nine years and England had entered a new era. It was a time of the awakening of the mind of the people.

The passing of the Reform Bill a little earlier had given the parliamentary franchise to many new voters, who began to realise their citizenship. The penny post had made intercourse easier, and the new railways were promoting travel, though as yet there was no through line from London to Scotland; people would go from the capital to Liverpool and then take ship to Glasgow.

There was a new independence of spirit among the working people, and the Chartists were agitating for rights which have now for the most part been fully conceded. All was not well in England. Those were "the Hungry Forties", and in many a poor home there was want bordering on starvation because of the scarcity and high price of bread. Cobden and Bright were advocating the repeal of the Corn Laws, which kept foreign corn out of the land, and they triumphed on the 25th June, 1846, when Sir Robert Peel secured from Parliament the passing of the Anti-Corn Law Bill, which inaugurated Free Trade. In this historic event two young politicians, destined to fame, took part, though on opposite sides – Gladstone and Disraeli.

It was a time when the conscience of the nation was beginning to be sensitive to the wrongs inflicted on the weak by cruel conditions of labour. Lord Shaftesbury was leading a crusade on behalf of little children employed in factories at an age when they ought to have been in the playground or the nursery, and for boy-sweeps compelled to climb chimneys and thus often to become cripples for life. This crusade issued in the Factory Act of 1847.

In the field of religion, too, stirring events were taking place. The Disruption of 1843 had drawn from the Church of Scotland a band of men and women, led by Thomas Chalmers, to form the Free Church of Scotland; and in England in

1845 the Tractarian Movement had issued in the secession from the Anglican Church to Rome of a group of High Churchmen, headed by John Henry Newman. There is no doubt that this event, drawing attention to the beliefs and claims of the Roman Catholic Church, tended to arouse in the Protestants of this land a realisation of the danger to be apprehended from the Papacy and the need for Protestants to draw together for the strength that comes from unity.

The continent of Europe in 1846 was full of unrest. Thrones were tottering under the shock of the political discontents that brought about the revolutions of 1848, in France, Italy and Germany.

In heathen lands the modern missionary movement was making itself felt. In India the pioneer, William Carey, had passed away, but Alexander Duff and John Wilson were carrying his work forward in a great educational campaign. China, which had been closed to foreigners, was opening its doors a little way, and in 1842 five Treaty ports had been made available to people of other lands, among whom missionaries came eagerly forward. Japan was as yet a closed land. In Africa Moffat was working among the Bechuanas and his son-in-law, Livingstone, was moving north from South Africa towards the dark, slavery-cursed region of Central Africa, "beckoned" by "the smoke of a thousand villages". In the Pacific Islands, visited a little before by Charles Darwin, murderers and cannibals were being won for Christ by the successors of the martyred John Williams.

It was a time that called everywhere for the influence of a united and powerful Christian Church.

CHAPTER II

BIRTH OF THE ALLIANCE

(a) Preparations. In 1846 the churches of the various denominations in Great Britain were largely separated from one another in life and work, but the need of unity was making itself felt and was finding expression in many quarters. In 1843 the bicentenary of the Westminster Assembly was being celebrated in Scotland and Dr. Balmer, of Berwick, pleaded for a closer unity among Christians. His plea deeply impressed John Henderson, a wealthy merchant, of Park, near Glasgow, and he resolved to do something towards bringing Christians together. With a view to this, he asked a number of leading ministers, of different denominations but known to favour unity, to write essays on the subject for publication. All thus invited consented to write, among them being Drs. Chalmers and Candlish of the Free Church of Scotland; John Angell James, the Congregational minister of Carr's Lane, Birmingham, and Dr. King, John Henderson's own minister. The essays were published in a volume entitled *Essays on Christian Union*, and helped to stimulate British opinion.

Not only in Britain was this movement stirring. In 1843 Dr. Patton, of New York, wrote to John Angell James, suggesting that a conference of delegates from different denominations should be convened in London to set forth the truths on which they were agreed. Extracts from this American letter were printed by Mr. James as an appendix to his contribution to *Essays on Christian Union*.

In continental Europe also the wind of the Spirit was blowing at this time. In Switzerland Dr. Merle D'Aubigne, the historian of the Reformation, invited his brethren to form a fraternal confederation, while in Germany, Belgium and France the Archdeacon of Danzig made a tour in order to promote friendship among Christians of different Churches, established or free.

It was now felt that the time had come to bring the matter before the public in London, and a meeting was arranged in Exeter Hall, Strand, in June, 1843. The response was overwhelming. Such was the demand for tickets that eleven thousand were issued, three times the number of persons the hall would hold. Long before the hour the great building was thronged and crowds went away disappointed. Among the speakers at this memorable gathering were Dr. James Hamilton, the Hon. and Rev. Baptist Noel, and John Angell James. The speakers had not to convince the audience, but to guide and direct their enthusiasm. It was made clear that night that the movement towards unity had the support, not only of Christian leaders, but of the rank and file.

Again, a lead forward came from Scotland. In the summer of 1845, a letter prepared by a group of Scotsmen was sent to Evangelical clergy and ministers in England, Wales and Ireland, referring to the proposal for a London Conference, and urging that a preparatory Conference should be held that autumn in Liverpool. This was approved and 216 Church leaders, drawn from twenty denominations, met in the Medical Hall, Liverpool, and drew up plans of procedure. The meetings lasted three days and were marked by the utmost friendliness and warmth. At one point indeed two Doctors of Divinity, the Chairman and another, were led to acknowledge an estrangement which had long divided them, but which in the atmosphere of that gathering they were resolved to dismiss for ever. Their utterances, spoken with emotion, deeply touched their fellow-members, who felt them to be signs of the working in their midst of the Spirit of divine love.

It was resolved at this Conference to recommend the forming of an "Evangelical Alliance" and, in preparation for it, to hold a series of gatherings in great cities. This was accordingly done, and meetings were organised in Dublin, Belfast, Manchester, Newcastle and Birmingham. Multitudes assembled in these centres such as to crowd the largest halls. In Manchester, for example, the Free Trade Hall was taken and was thronged an hour before the time with an audience eager for Christian fellowship.

It must not, however, he supposed that there were no critics of the movement. Archbishop Whately, of Dublin, thought that the members of the Alliance would defeat their own object, "by producing more dissension than union". He therefore admonished the clergy of his diocese to avoid its associations and deposed a curate who disobeyed him.

The *Christian Witness* and the *Christian Observer*, though both Evangelical, assailed the proposed Alliance. Dr. Campbell, a prominent Nonconformist, attacked the new movement in the *Christian Witness* on the ground that it proposed "to achieve impossibilities". This, of course, remained to be seen, and the advocates of a closer unity went on with their campaign. As the Baptist, John Howard Hinton, said, in words made his own by the Wesleyan, Dr. Bunting, "Whatever tempests may beset its course, I would rather go to sea in this little bark and risk the perishing in it, than stand upon the shore, an idle or an indifferent spectator".

At Birmingham, in April, 1846, it was resolved that a General Conference should be held in London during the coming August. For the expenses of this Conference a fund of £6,000 was raised – and raised quickly and with enthusiasm. The intention had been to have a British Conference, but an appeal came from the United States that the membership should be open to people of other lands, and this was agreed.

So the field was set for the great day.

(b) Formation. On Wednesday, 19th August, 1846, the General Conference assembled in the Freemasons' Hall, Great Queen Street, London. There were from 800 to 1,000 Christian leaders – ministers, professors, laymen – many of high degree. As one of them, Dr. J. W. Massie, remarks in his record of the event, "The roll of members present will bear comparison with the councils of early fathers, the ecclesiastical diets of the later empire, or the synods and assemblies of the Papal Church". The facsimile signatures of those attending are preserved in a spacious volume at the Alliance headquarters and form a precious memento. There is the handwriting of men whose names in many cases are household words throughout the Christian Church – Bickersteth, Blackwood, Kinnaird – Binney, Angell James, Leifchild – Howard Hinton, Baptist Noel, Steane – Osborn and Bunting – Candlish and Buchanan – Tholuck, D'Aubigné, Adolphe Monod – Patton and S. H. Cox – John Henderson and Sir Culling Eardley. These came from all parts of the British Isles and from Germany, France, Switzerland, the United States and Canada, while they are said to have represented no less than fifty-two "bodies of Christians".

The Conference met for thirteen days, holding sessions morning and evening, with Committees in the afternoon. At the first session Sir Culling Eardley, Baronet, was elected to the chair and in the evening of the day his chairmanship was confirmed for the entire period of the Conference. It is clear that his firm but kindly guidance contributed much to the success of the assembly.

Every session opened with a brief devotional service, which gave tone to the proceedings. Indeed, the spirit of the gatherings was shown by an incident which took place between the first day's sessions. Many of the members of the Conference dined together and directly after the removal of the cloth it was proposed that one of Watts's hymns should be sung. "Come, let us join our cheerful songs" was struck up and sung with great heartiness. Many foreign brethren were there and it was now suggested that hymns in German and French should be sung. A translation of every two lines was given, and it is said that the interruption did not detract from the enthusiasm. The effect is said to have been electrical. All seemed to join in the spirit and to regard the moment as a foretaste of the harmony and joy of heaven.

CHRISTIAN UNITY

On the second day the Conference passed a resolution, declaring that it had met, not to create Christian union, but to confess the unity which the Church of Christ possessed as His Body. In moving the resolution Dr. Wardlaw expressed his belief, which was evidently that of the assembly, that when a sinner accepted Christ as his Saviour he became a member of the Lord's body and became at the same moment one with all who were of Christ throughout the earth.

FORMATION AND NAME OF THE ALLIANCE

In the evening of the same day Dr. Buchanan moved "that the members of this Conference are deeply convinced of the desirableness of forming a confederation, on the basis of great evangelical principles held in common by them, which may afford opportunity to members of the Church of Christ of cultivating brotherly love, enjoying Christian intercourse, and promoting such other objects as they may hereafter agree to prosecute together; and they hereby proceed to form such a confederation, under the name of '*The Evangelical Alliance*'." Before the vote was taken Sir Culling Eardley asked all to stand and spend a few moments in silent prayer. This was done and the resolution was then passed unanimously. An extraordinary scene followed. The members of the infant Alliance, filled with joy, exchanged greetings by shaking hands with one another, Churchman with Nonconformist, Calvinist with Arminian, Briton with foreigner. It was felt to be "a jubilee of union and a time of sanguine hope".

THE DOCTRINAL BASIS

On the third day the Rev. E. Bickersteth proposed the doctrinal basis of the Alliance. This caused long discussion and several amendments, but was passed after three days in the following form:

"That the parties composing the Alliance shall be such persons only as hold and maintain what are usually understood to be Evangelical views, in regard to the matters of doctrine understated, namely:

1. The divine Inspiration, Authority and Sufficiency of the Holy Scriptures.
2. The Right and Duty of Private Judgment in the Interpretation of the Holy Scriptures.
3. The Unity of the Godhead, and the Trinity of Persons therein.
4. The utter Depravity of Human Nature, in consequence of the Fall.
5. The Incarnation of the Son of God, His work of Atonement for sinners of mankind, and His Mediatorial Intercession and Reign.
6. The Justification of the sinner by Faith alone.
7. The work of the Holy Spirit in the Conversion and Sanctification of the sinner.
8. The Immortality of the Soul, the Resurrection of the Body, the Judgment of the World by our Lord Jesus Christ, with the Eternal Blessedness of the Righteous, and the Eternal Punishment of the Wicked.

9. The divine Institution of the Christian Ministry, and the obligation and perpetuity of the Ordinances of Baptism and the Lord's Supper.

    (i)   It is, however, distinctly declared that this brief summary is not to be regarded, in any formal or ecclesiastical sense, as a creed or confession, nor the adoption of it as involving an assumption of the right authoritatively to define the limits of Christian brotherhood.
    (ii)   In this Alliance it is also distinctly declared that no compromise of the views of any member, or sanction of those of others on the points wherein they differ, is either required or expected; but that all are held free as before to maintain and advocate their religious convictions with due forbearance and brotherly love.
    (iii)   It is not contemplated that this Alliance should assume or aim at the character of a new ecclesiastical organisation, claiming and exercising the functions of a Christian Church. Its simple and comprehensive object, it is strongly felt, may be successfully promoted without interfering with, or disturbing the order of, any branch of the Christian Church to which its members may respectively belong."

This basis having been passed nem. con., the Conference sang, with deep, devotional feeling, the hymn

> "All hail the Great Immanuel's Name,
> Let Angels prostrate fall."

THE QUESTION OF SLAVERY

Before the Conference closed a question arose which might have split the Alliance. Many of the British members wished a resolution passed that no slave-holder should be received as a member. Most of the Americans, while agreeing in detestation of slavery, were unwilling to pass this regulation as it would prevent American churches in fellowship with churches including slave-holders from coming in and the Alliance would be seriously limited. After days of debate it was agreed not to make anti-slavery a part of the constitution of the Alliance, but to confine the basis to the spiritual principles which had brought the members together, while all would be free to follow the dictates of conscience in this matter.

We in this later day realise the cost at which, through a terrible Civil War, the United States was to extinguish slavery from its midst.

The attitude of the whole Conference to the negro race was shown in a striking episode towards the close of the sessions. On the morning of the last day a negro minister entered the hall. He was Mollison Maddison Clark, pastor of a coloured church composed chiefly of slaves, situated in Washington, in sight of the Capitol and the slave auction stand. He had left America to attend the Conference, but his ship had met with a disaster which had prevented his arriving earlier. His personality impressed the assembly and he was invited to speak. Tall and erect, of handsome face and easy manner, he secured attention at once and his speech confirmed the first impression. Expressing his sense of the value of the newly-formed Alliance and of his privilege in being admitted to its membership, he said, "Representing, as I do, over 17,000 professing Christians in the United States of America, members of the African Methodist Episcopal denomination and, more or less remotely, three millions of my race, I feel the sacred and high honour, as well as the great responsibility." He went on to speak of the unity of his people with the Christian Church throughout the world, and their loyalty to its ideals and beliefs.

The response of the Conference was immediate and warm. One after another of the most distinguished Americans invited Mr. Clark to their homes and pulpits, and the Chairman gave him the right hand of fellowship.

WHAT IS THE ALLIANCE TO DO?

Dr. Thomas Chalmers had expressed himself afraid of a "union without work", and the Conference before ending defined the work it set itself. Its great object was to be the promotion of Christian unity, and in furtherance of this the members would: (1) seek to deepen in their own hearts the consciousness of their failure in the spirit of love, and would implore, through the merits and intercession of the Saviour, forgiveness of past sin in this respect and divine grace to lead them to the cultivation of that brotherly affection which is enjoined on all who, loving the Lord Jesus Christ, are bound also to love one another. (2) They would also endeavour to manifest the unity which exists among the disciples of Christ, by promoting fraternal and devotional intercourse, by discouraging all envyings, strifes and divisions, and by impressing upon Christians a deeper sense of the duty of obeying the Lord's command to "love one another" and so to seek the full accomplishment of His prayer, "That they all may be one, as Thou, Father, art in me and I in Thee; that they also may be one in us; that the world may believe that Thou hast sent Me". (3) They would open correspondence with Christian brethren in different parts of the world, especially with those who might be engaged, amidst peculiar difficulties and opposition, in the course of the Gospel, in order to afford them encouragement and sympathy and to diffuse an interest in their welfare. (4) The Alliance would endeavour to promote the advancement of Evangelical Protestantism and the counter-action of infidelity, Romanism and other forms of error and profaneness opposed to it, especially the desecration of the Lord's Day: it being understood that the different organisations of the Alliance would be left to adopt such methods of prosecuting these ends as might seem best to them: all at the same time pursuing them in the spirit of compassion and love.

These decisions, in substance, became known as "The Practical Resolutions", and as years went on were read and emphasised at every General Conference of the Alliance.

On September 2nd, the thirteenth day of its deliberations, the assembly closed in an atmosphere of thanksgiving and joy. The last session was lit up by the presentation of an address, in the French language, by the Continental members, in which gratitude was expressed to the British brethren for the inauguration of the Alliance and the hospitality shown throughout its sessions: also to the Chairman and others who had rendered special service. In closing, they saluted the American and all other members of the Conference, and commended the new Alliance to the grace and blessing of God. This address was signed by Adolphe Monod, F. A. G. Tholuck, C. Baup, Charles Cook and F. Martin.

It was felt that the Spirit of God had created among men a new and precious fellowship. In coming nearer to one another the members had come closer to the Lord Jesus. "The hours spent in our Conferences," said E. Bickersteth, "have been among the happiest of my life."

The Alliance had started on its way.

CHAPTER III

THE ALLIANCE BRANCHING OUT

THE Alliance, once established, at once began, like a vigorous tree, to put forth branches. First among these was that of

FRANCE

During the week of the founding of the Alliance the French members of the Conference came together and constituted themselves a Provisional Committee for the purpose of forming a branch of the Alliance in France, Belgium, French-speaking Switzerland and other populations using the French language.

The members of this Committee returned to their homes and consulted friends. Many were favourable; some doubtful; a few opposed. "After all," wrote one French leader, "the best answer we can make to our opponents is that which a certain philosopher made to a Sophist who denied Motion; *he walked*. We also walk, 'We walk in love, as Christ also hath loved us'."

The branch was formed and became a fruitful one. Belgium and French Switzerland formed themselves into sections of the French branch.

GERMANY

Germany was not long in following suit. Early in 1847 a branch was formed for North Germany, through the initiative of Herr Kuntze, of Berlin.

South Germany was more deliberate, but in the spring of 1847, at a Pastoral Conference there, strong sympathy with the Alliance was expressed, and in the autumn, after another Conference, Pastor Bonnet, of Frankfort, wrote, "I rejoice to say that the spirit of the Alliance is widely spreading all over Germany". There were, however, opponents in Germany, and a few months later a rationalistic journal triumphed over what it called "the extinguishment of the Evangelical Alliance", whose "meteoric light" had evidently shone on the rationalistic sky as a star of evil omen. Such an utterance is a testimony to the growing power of the Alliance, which was creating alarm in the ranks of unbelief. The later history of the Alliance in Germany was to give the best answer to the suggestion of an extinguished light.

CANADA

In November, 1846, a public meeting was held in Montreal, to receive a report from M. Richey who had attended the London Conference. After hearing this report the assembly resolved that it was desirable to form a North American branch, and this was done with enthusiasm.

UNITED STATES

In May, 1847, the United States delegates to the London Conference and other Christian leaders met in New York and prepared a document laying down the principles to govern an American branch of the Alliance and inviting Christians who approved this to join the proposed fellowship. The Committee now appointed was to meet every week to receive applications. The organisation of the branch went on successfully.

SWEDEN

A group of Christian leaders, in April, 1847, issued a paper telling of the birth of the Alliance as "one of the most important events in the history of the Protestant Church" and inviting Swedish Christians to unite in a Swedish branch. A letter from Gothenburg tells of the growth of the spirit of unity and a little later a branch of the Alliance was formed at Christiansand.

INDIA

In 1849 a meeting of Christian workers was held at Agra, at which it was resolved to form a branch of the Alliance.

This was done and a Committee of Management, with a Secretary, appointed. Thus the light of the Alliance began to shine in a great heathen land.

TURKEY

In 1855 a branch was formed in Constantinople, public meetings being held in Pera and keen interest displayed.

SPAIN

In Spain, after many years of Protestant witness and frequent persecution by the authorities, a branch of the Alliance was established. Practically all the leading Evangelical workers in Spain united in it, holding joint prayer meetings in the cities every month. In this way the Alliance came to be regarded by the Spanish Government as the voice of all Spanish Evangelicals and its representations were listened to with respect and consideration.

PORTUGAL

In Portugal also, in spite of Romanist opposition, a branch of the Alliance was set up and became strong, carrying on a many-sided Evangelical work, to which fuller reference will be made in a later chapter.

It would take far too long, however, to detail the formation of all the branches which were more or less fully organised as years went by. They are scattered throughout the world – in all the continents and many of the islands of the sea. It is now truly "THE WORLD'S EVANGELICAL ALLIANCE".

CHAPTER IV

MILESTONES OF ADVANCE

THE progress of the Alliance during its first fifty years may best be checked by the General Conferences which stand out as milestones by the way.

The first of these is that of

LONDON, 1851

This year is famous for the great International Exhibition in London, when the Crystal Palace in Hyde Park was the resort of millions of visitors from our own and other lands. The brilliant display of art and industry, and the social contacts day by day of a throng speaking many languages, kindled new hopes of friendship and co-operation between the nations of the earth.

The Evangelical Alliance saw in the occasion a grand opportunity, and a General Conference was held in Freemasons' Hall, the birthplace of the Alliance, attended in addition to Britishers by 30 delegates from France, 47 from Germany, 40 from Switzerland, 22 from Holland, 13 from Belgium, 6 from Sweden, 22 from the United States, and individuals from Russia, the West and East Indies, China and other lands.

At this Conference a notable address on the "Practical Resolutions" of the Alliance was delivered by E. H. Bickersteth, Curate of Banningham, Norfolk, who later became Bishop of Exeter and is well known as the author of the hymn "Peace, perfect peace". Referring to his father, one of the chief founders of the Alliance, who in the meantime bad passed away, Mr. Bickersteth pictured the larger fellowship in heaven and on earth, and closed with lines composed by himself:

"Thus heaven is gathering, one by one, in its capacious breast,
All that is pure and permanent, and beautiful and blest;

> The family is scattered yet, though of one home and heart,
> Part militant in earthly gloom, in heavenly glory part,
> But who can speak the rapture, when the circle is complete,
> And all the children, sundered now, before their Father meet;
> One fold, one shepherd, one employ, one everlasting Home–
> 'Lo, I come quickly'; Even so, Amen, Lord Jesus, come."

Dr. King, one of the founders, gave a vivid account of the 1846 Conference and of the progress made since – of the shield it had placed around the persecuted for Christ's sake, of its battles with infidelity, Popery and Sabbath desecration, and, especially, of the gatherings in Jamaica in which a recently-emancipated people welcomed missionaries of many societies to "a former scene of slavery", "transformed by divine grace," said Dr. King, "into a seat of glorious liberty and a paradise of God".

The Conference revealed the Alliance as entering into its stride and realising its strength. Its members went back to their homes with a quickened sense of call and opportunity, and with the ringing words of Dr. James Hamilton on "The Final Triumph of the Church of Christ" echoing in their hearts.

PARIS, 1855

This was the first International Conference of the Alliance held out of England and in a Roman Catholic country. It was convened by the French branch of the Alliance and was attended by some 1,200 persons drawn from fifteen nations.

Queen Victoria was at the time visiting the French Emperor, and the President of the Conference, Dr. Grandpierre, in welcoming the guests, exclaimed with emotion, "*Que les temps sont changés!* Three hundred years ago and a little more, in this very month (August), almost on this very day, occurred the massacre of St. Bartholomew; and now our Emperor welcomes to his palace, as his honoured guest, the Protestant Queen of a great Protestant nation; while we, descendants of the martyred Huguenots of those days, are assembled in this capital, to receive our brethren, not of France only, but of the whole world".

The meetings continued on a high level for ten days, one of the most important sessions being the one devoted to the question of religious liberty. Cases of persecution in several lands were reported, with the steps taken by the Alliance to counter them. The Conference closed with a Communion Service, in which the words of the Lord Jesus over the bread and the wine were pronounced in seven languages – French, English, German, Dutch, Italian, Swedish and Danish.

BERLIN, 1857

The Conference in Berlin was a notable one. It began with a service in the great Garrison Church, by permission of the King of Prussia, at whose command the cathedral choir rendered Mendelssohn's Hundredth Psalm as the opening act.

The usual programme of addresses was varied by a unique item on the Saturday afternoon, when the entire Conference was received at Potsdam by the King (Frederick William IV). About 900 guests arrived by special trains provided at the King's expense, and on entering the palace found refreshments prepared, after partaking of which they moved out into the garden, on the terrace of which the speech-making was to take place. Addresses to the King from Sir Culling Eardley and others followed, in his reply to which His Majesty expressed his deep interest in the Alliance, saying, "I have always felt the most earnest desire to promote such a union among Christians, and hitherto it has appeared to me impossible, but now I rejoice to see it. The first step is taken. The first days of the Conference are passed, with the joy and blessing of the Lord. I trust it will be the same with the rest. My wish and most fervent prayer is that there may descend upon all the members of the Conference an effusion of the Spirit of God, like that which fell on the first disciples at Pentecost".

The ladies had meanwhile been accommodated with chairs on the steps of the terrace, and a list of their names had been taken to the Queen. When the King had begun his proceedings, the Queen, attended by maids of honour, passed along the line of ladies, bowing to all and speaking to many.

At the close, when their Majesties were moving to leave, the assembly struck up Luther's hymn, "Ein feste Burg ist unser Gott", singing one verse. Then a minister from within the palace stepped forward and offered a short prayer, closing with the Benediction. The King and Queen stopped when they heard the first notes of the hymn and remained till the end of the prayer.

The last service of this Berlin Conference was a memorable one, according to the account of it given by the famous Scots preacher, Robertson of Irvine. It was held in the Garrison Church, holding 3,000 and on this occasion crowded with a brilliant assemblage, including the King and Queen. Words of thanks and farewell were spoken by Dean Alford, of Canterbury, in "a silvery stream"; by Dr. Patton, of New York, "a stalwart, kingly-looking man"; and by M. le Pasteur Fisch, from Paris. The concluding address was delivered by Dr. Krummacher, a court-preacher of Germany. One special outcome of this Conference was the Sunday School movement, which has since spread so widely in the Fatherland.

GENEVA, 1861

The Geneva Conference, convened by the French branch of the Alliance, was opened in the ancient Cathedral of St. Pierre. Pasteur G. Monod, of Paris, in speaking, referred to the associations of Geneva, first with the Christian Reformer, Calvin, and then with the sceptical Voltaire. "Who," asked M. Monod, "would have said a hundred years ago that such a meeting as this would be held in Geneva, and that the greatest number of deputies would come from the countries of Gibbon, Voltaire and Frederick II. ...? The age of the Encyclopedists, which ended in blood, has produced the era of the Bible Societies."

Stress was laid in this Conference on the importance of Evangelistic work outside the churches. In advocating this, Baptist Noel referred to the value of contact with the people which such work brought, even though at first the hearers might be offended. "One day," he said, "I was preaching in the open air, when a half-drunken man addressed me: 'Did you ever see God?' I answered, 'I am not a brute: I can believe what I do not see.' Those round about tried to silence the man. 'I suppose you will put me in prison?' said he. 'No. I want to let you out.' The people took hold of him and prayed for him."

In one session an Italian speaker, dealing with liberty, quoted Garibaldi as saying: "The Bible is the cannon which will free Italy."

The total number of members at this Conference was 1,887, of whom 647 belonged to Geneva itself. One result of this Conference was the giving of a stimulus to the better observance of the Lord's Day.

TERCENTENARY OF THE DEATH OF CALVIN

Between the "Milestone" Conferences of Geneva (1861) and Amsterdam (1867) there took place Conferences of a special nature – celebrating the tercentenary of the death of John Calvin. Calvin died on the 27th May, 1564, and the Geneva Branch of the Alliance now appealed to the British organisation for the holding, in 1864, of a commemorative celebration.

This was arranged and on 29th May, 1864, a Calvin Commemoration gathering was held in the Freemasons' Hall, London. The chair was occupied by Lord Calthorpe, and addresses were delivered by Messrs. T. R. Birks, Baptist Noel, W. Arthur and Dr. T. M'Crie.

A fuller celebration was felt to be appropriate in Geneva, whose debt to Calvin was realised as unique. Conferences were therefore held there during the week, May 22–29, in which tributes were paid to the great Reformer who, beside teaching his doctrines of predestination, the spiritual presence only in the Ordinance of the Lord's Supper, and the independence of the Christian Church, reformed the civil government of the city, established an academy, fostered literature and science, and made Geneva "the metropolis of the Reformed faith".

Gatherings of commemoration were also held in Paris and Edinburgh.

AMSTERDAM, 1867

Dr. Steane, writing of this Conference, notes the kindly hospitality shown by the Dutch. At the railway station the first thing that caught the eye of the traveller was a large banner bearing the words "Evangelical Alliance" in different languages. Surrounding it were gentlemen wearing the tricolour of Holland round their hats. These gentlemen welcomed the arrivals, directing them to an office in which each was presented with a map of the city, a programme of the Conference and the address of his host and hostess.

The inaugural service was held in the cathedral, some 3,000 to 4,000 being present. The preacher was Prof. Van Oosterzee, of the University of Utrecht, who showed himself a "master of oratory"; his subject being "The Communion of Saints" (Acts xviii. 14, 15).

At one of the sessions Dr. Guthrie, well known for his work for "Ragged Schools", presided and, in paying a graceful tribute to Holland, recalled the influence of William the Silent and William III in the fostering of Evangelical liberty. In addition to the regular sessions, meetings in halls and in the open air were held, and addressed by Lord Radstock and General Alexander on "The Common Salvation". Also a great missionary meeting at Vogelensang, when 12,000 persons were said to be present.

It is interesting to note that years afterwards Count Bernstorff affirmed that this Conference gave rise to a great Evangelistic movement in Holland.

NEW YORK, 1873

The Conference at New York was described as "the largest, the happiest, and most influential of the General Conferences up to that time convened by the Evangelical Alliance". The reception given to their guests by the Americans was enthusiastic and lavish. The gatherings filled the largest buildings in New York and some overflowed them. General Grant, President of the United States, welcomed the delegates, at the White House, in Washington, "to the capital of this great nation which," he said, "I feel is the freest to work out the problem of your mission".

The chair at the sessions was taken by the Hon. W. E. Dodge, President of the American branch of the Alliance. Owing to the overwhelming attendances, it was found necessary for the Conference to meet in sections. At one of these the theme was "The Pulpit and the Age", two of the speakers being Joseph Parker and Henry Ward Beecher.

Dr. John Stoughton, in speaking of Protestant relations between America and Europe, told of the beginnings of Methodism in the States – in 1766 a German Irishman, who had been brought back to God through Wesley, opening his house in New York for Methodist worship; and three years later an appeal for preachers being sent to Wesley. The Methodist Conference was then sitting at Leeds, England. "Who is willing to go?" asked Wesley. Two earnest itinerants, named Boardman and Pilmoor, answered, each of them, "Here am I, send me". "Thus", added Stoughton, "the Methodism of America became engrafted on the English stock."

The impression left by this Conference in New York may be gauged by the words of the *New York Observer* in reviewing it: "The most remarkable religious convention that the world ever saw is now part of the history of the Church of God."

BASLE, 1879

The Conference at Basle was strongly influenced by the historical associations of the city. Here it found itself among reminders of Erasmus and Oecolampadius; here in the great hall of the Münster was held the celebrated Council of Basle (1431–1448), which a hundred years before the Reformation discussed schemes for the purification of the Church from errors and abuses.

But besides memories of a great past, the Conference found a living and warm fellowship in the things of Christ. The numbers attending were greater than ever before, except at New York; the chief languages of the week were German and French, with English taking a minor place.

The connection with England was, however, recalled by Dr. Stoughton, who, as an historian, reminded the Conference of the refuge given in Basle to English exiles during the time of persecution in England; among those sheltered being Bishop Hooper, of Gloucester. The coming to Basle of Hooper, his wife and little daughter Rachel in an old-fashioned carriage, and later their departure by boat on the Rhine, with the waving of handkerchiefs to friends at Basle who had shown hospitality, were vividly described, with a touch of pathos caused by the remembrance of Hooper's subsequent martyrdom. At this Conference it was resolved to appoint an International Committee to whom would be entrusted the duty of taking steps to secure religious liberty in lands where it was violated. A resolution of protest against the opium traffic was also passed, calling upon England to change her policy with regard to it.

The Times of London devoted a leading article to the Conference, paying tribute to the Alliance and to the practical work linked by it with Evangelical doctrine. Referring to the spokesmen of the Alliance, *The Times* said, "What they say is listened to, and what they purpose will be eagerly watched and aided, by a vast band of sympathisers in every country, and not least in our own. The Evangelical Alliance is triumphant about the past, and has, even more, good hope about the future."

It is stated that the Basle Assembly was specially marked by the spirit of prayer, and that the result of this was seen in a great increase of prayer meetings in connection with the Universal Week of Prayer.

COPENHAGEN, 1884

The Copenhagen Conference had a stamp of novelty in that it brought the Scandinavian group of nations into the field of Alliance operations for the first time to any perceptible degree. Its meetings were rendered delightful by the kindness of the Danes, whose King and Queen, accompanied by the Crown Prince and Princess and other members of the Royal Family, showed their interest by attendance at the Congress. "It was a unique sight," remarked Mr. A. J. Arnold, "to see an ex-Lord Mayor of London, Sir William McArthur (a Wesleyan Methodist), presiding over one of the meetings, and cordially welcoming the presence of the Royal Family of the country."

At one of the sessions Dr. Underhill, Secretary of the Baptist Missionary Society, made grateful reference to the protection given by a former King of Denmark to Carey and his co-workers at the Danish settlement of Serampore, at a time when British India, under the East India Company, had no room for missionaries to the Indian people. A resolution

The New York (U.S.A.) Conference 1873
Group on the steps of the Capitol, Washington (see page 30)

The Amsterdam Conference of the Alliance, 1867 (see page 29)

was unanimously passed by the Conference expressing appreciation of this great service rendered by Denmark to the missionary cause.

Detailed reports of Christian work in many lands were given, with news of the growth of religious liberty, though here, strangely enough, an exception was found in Switzerland, where fierce attacks had been made on the newly-arrived Salvation Army. Against these attacks the Conference made protest.

One feature revealed in the religious situation, however, is one which we of a later date can understand only too well. Principal Cairns, of Scotland, in giving his impressions of the Conference, tells of one of the debates in which evidence was given of the terrible crisis through which Christianity was passing in its conflict with error and darkness in all the leading nations of the world. Dr. Cairns was so depressed by it that a shadow was cast for him over the otherwise exhilarating excursion later in the day to Roskilde. Here the Conference visited the ancient cathedral, the Westminster Abbey of Denmark, and songs of faith and praise broke forth. To Cairns, however, the tall pillars of the lonely cathedral by the sea seemed, as they reverberated with majestic Christian music, to gather around them the mocking spirits of darkness.

So in 1884 the battle of to-day was already being fought in Europe!

FLORENCE, 1891

Peculiar interest attached to this Conference held in the heart of Roman Catholic Italy, and in the city in which, forty years earlier the Grand Duke of Tuscany had cruelly persecuted Protestant Christians. The President of the Florence Committee, Dr. Geymonat, had himself been imprisoned in those dark days. Well might he close his address of welcome by asking: "Is it really in Italy, in Florence, only a few steps from Savonarola's wood-pile and the Bargello that we are assembled? . . . Is it really in Florence where the Madiai for the sake of the Gospel in August 1851 were arrested, and in June 1852 condemned for years to the galleys, where an honoured deputation of the Evangelical Alliance came to implore from the Grand Duke their liberation and could not obtain an official hearing? Yet on this very spot we open this free

Conference of Evangelicals of all nations! Scarcely can we believe our eyes."

The first act of the Conference was to send a telegram to King Humbert, thanking him for his kind recognition of the assembly, and a cordial reply came from His Majesty, in which he acknowledged "with great satisfaction the salutation and the homage of the representatives of the religious faith professed by the Piedmontese region so dear to his heart and so loyal to his throne".

The sessions which followed grew in attendance until the large theatre was crowded, and as this theatre could not be taken for less than a month it was decided to utilise it for Gospel services after the Conference. These services prove a wonderful success. On Sundays and three days during the week the theatre was filled with working people, nearly all Roman Catholics, and at the close of the month the theatre was secured for a second month, the services being conducted by ministers and laymen of different Evangelical Churches. A bit of practical Alliance work!

The Florence Conference and its sequel showed to Roman Catholic Italy that Protestants, often thought to be hopelessly divided, were really one in Christ and could meet in brotherly fellowship and co-operation.

LONDON, 1896

The General Conferences of the first fifty years of Alliance history came to a climax in the Jubilee gatherings in London. These began on Monday, June 29th, at Exeter Hall, with a largely-attended Prayer Meeting, followed by an International Conversazione and a great evening meeting, with Lord Polwarth, the President of the British Alliance, in the chair. The hall was decorated with palms, ferns and flowering plants, while across the front of the organ hung a banner bearing the familiar motto of the Alliance: "Unum Corpus Sumus In Christo."

The first act of the Conference was to give praise to God for His good hand upon the Alliance throughout the half-century of its history. This was done through a resolution proposed by the Bishop of Exeter and carried with deep feeling, A brief sketch of the history of the Alliance, entitled

"These Fifty Years", was presented by its Secretary, Mr. A. J. Arnold, after which the foreign visitors were welcomed and many of them replied in short, trenchant speeches.

It was happily noted that two of the leaders present – Dr. Joseph Angus and Dr. Newman Hall – were links with the earliest days, having been among the founders.

During the remaining days of the Conference, the Alliance joined with the Mildmay Conference, a sister-body founded by the Rev. W. Pennefather, a member of the Alliance Council; and the joint meetings took place in the Mildmay Conference Hall. Here three sessions were held daily and the beautiful grounds surrounding the hall promoted social intercourse. On the lawn were two large tents in which luncheon and tea were served, and meetings under the famous "Mulberry Tree" proved specially popular. "Thursday was perhaps," as a transatlantic writer suggested, "the most interesting of all the days of the Jubilee." The subject was "The Unity of the Church Perfected in Glory".

On the Friday afternoon a United Communion service was attended by nearly two thousand persons.

On the Sunday preceding the Conference, sermons on Christian Unity were preached in more than a hundred churches and chapels of London, and Westminster Abbey and St. Paul's Cathedral came into the celebration by welcoming foreign guests. At the Abbey, Dean Bradley received a company of them in the Jerusalem Chamber before the Conference began; and on another day, at St. Paul's, the Archdeacon of London welcomed a hundred, afterwards entertaining them to tea in the Chapter House.

The Bishop of Exeter, a Vice-President of the Alliance, invited the chief foreign visitors to Exeter as guests at the Palace, where they met a large number of the clergy and ministers of the diocese.

In Liverpool also the Jubilee was celebrated, with special appropriateness as the preliminary Conference to prepare for the founding of the Alliance had been held there in 1845. In Dublin a similar meeting was held, as also at some foreign branches, including Shanghai.

Clearly, the Jubilee Conference set the seal of God upon the Alliance as an instrument in the divine Hand for accomplishing the purposes for which the Gospel is given.

CHAPTER V

THE ALLIANCE AND PRAYER

1. *The Universal Week of Prayer.* From the beginning of the Evangelical Alliance, prayer has been the secret and inspiration of its life, and it has laid stress on the need of prayer as essential to everything good. With this in mind it has appealed for special and united prayer during the first week of each year, desiring thus to encourage a habit and obtain a grace for the hallowing of the entire year.

The appeal for the week is issued during the latter half of the preceding year, and was at first sent out to a circle in comparatively intimate touch with the London headquarters, but a group of missionaries in Ludhiana (India), in 1860, petitioned the Council to extend the call to all parts of the world. This was gladly done and so the week became the Universal Week of Prayer.

In preparation for the Week a letter, signed by representative Christian leaders, is sent out, accompanied by a programme of topics for prayer suggested for the different days. The letter and programme are translated into about a hundred languages, among which in this centennial year Hebrew is for the first time included.

The magnitude to which this has attained can be judged from the fact that in connection with the ninetieth year of the Alliance over a quarter of a million programmes in English alone were called for and despatched, in addition to which numerous foreign translations were furnished. Among the foreign languages are Greek, Arabic, Bengali, Hindi, Urdu, Japanese, Chinese, Siamese, Sinhalese, Swahili, Telugu, Kanarese, Luganda and Zulu.

Noonday Prayer Meetings are held in churches, halls and mission houses in Central London, the opening one being often in the Mansion House, with the Lord Mayor presiding – an example followed in many other cities. Afternoon and evening gatherings take place in convenient buildings throughout Great Britain and numerous other lands. The week has in several recent years been inaugurated by an address broadcast from the B.B.C. headquarters. In the meetings for prayer all Protestant denominations unite and they are felt to be seasons of refreshing from the presence of the Lord.

Testimonies to the value of the Week of Prayer come from all quarters. From the minister-in-charge of the Church of Scotland Mission at Bandawa, Nyasaland, came the following: "Our union with the World's Evangelical Alliance has brought us great joy and blessings. Our topics held according to the appointment. On 12th January six congregations united. Our ingathering was noble, as the number of the communicants was 1,355 who shared the Lord's Table; the number at the General Meeting was uncountable. There was no room to hold them in the church, therefore the meetings were held in the open air. . . . May God bless His work through the Alliance, carried out round the globe!"

From Tiberias, by the Sea of Galilee: "We had real seasons of refreshment during the Universal Week of Prayer. No less than fifteen different nations were represented at our Prayer Meetings. As one heard the different tongues uniting in prayer to the One Heavenly Father, it seemed a foretaste of that day when that great multitude of all nations and kindreds and tongues shall stand before the Throne and before the Lamb joining in unison the triumph song of the redeemed."

And this from Kita, the Gold Coast: "The meetings were attended regularly, not only by Protestants, but also by Roman Catholics and Pagans. We felt that the Lord poured out His blessing on all who attended."

From Paris Dr. C. Merle D'Aubigne wrote that six of the large West End churches joined for meetings during the week of prayer, these taking place daily throughout the week, with large attendances.

Vivid accounts of the Week have come respecting China. The Rev. C. G. Sparham, a former missionary there, wrote: "In England very often it seemed to be the faithful few who gathered together for prayer. But in Central China the Week of Prayer was observed, from the time it was taken up at all, in the early eighties, as a festival of prayer. There was something of the zest about it than there is in the larger May meetings here in London . . . and there was an enthusiasm and a joy that it would be difficult to convey to an English audience."

In corroboration of this, Dr. Cheng Ching Yi has said: "Well do I remember in my boyhood days in North China (Pekin) that we always looked forward to that first week of the New Year, when all the Christian people gathered together for corporate intercession and prayer among the different Churches. Even till this day in many parts of China that week is regarded as a leading event in the life of the Christian Church of my country."

It is interesting to note that during the later years of the second Great War the last day of the Week of Prayer has been signalized in St. Paul's Cathedral, London, in a service attended by representatives of many nations, prayers being offered in their own languages by several, including, in 1943, the Archbishop of Thyatira. This service has been arranged by the World's Evangelical Alliance in conjunction with the Cathedral Chapter.

2. *War Prayer Meetings.* During the two great wars of 1914–18 and 1939–45 the Alliance arranged monthly Prayer Meetings to present the national cause before the Lord. Those in the earlier war were held in the spacious Queen's Hall, and were attended by audiences averaging some 2,500 persons, and sometimes quite filling the hall. National leaders took part in these gatherings, which were marked by deep feeling, Christian and patriotic, and constituted a memorable feature in a time of public and private trouble.

In the later war Queen's Hall was destroyed by enemy bombardment, but united Prayer Meetings were held in the Central Hall, Westminster, and later in the Caxton Hall. These gatherings also were impressive and influential. Leaders of many Churches and representatives of Parliament, the City of London and the War Services took part month by month, as well as members of the rank and file of the Churches. Sometimes a touch of humour brought a smile, as when the Recorder of London, in paying tribute to the patience and cheerfulness of humble Londoners in time of danger, told of an old and poor woman whose home had been damaged in the night by enemy bombs and who was engaged next morning in sweeping up the debris. A friend sympathised with her, but she replied, "Oh, there's nothing like a blitz to take your mind off the war". Even better, however, the audience felt, was such an assembly as the one in which they then were. Although the stillness of the meeting was sometimes broken by the sharp clap of a near explosion, there was a sense of the overshadowing Presence of God and we were in a pavilion of peace.

To promote the spirit of prayer among the general population, posters, prepared by the Alliance, were placed in the London Tube railways, some with a pictured clock-face showing the two hands pointed upward towards heaven at twelve o'clock, as a call to the "Noon Watch" prayer.

3. *Days of National Prayer*. During the recent war the Alliance Council was in repeated communication with the Prime Minister and the Archbishop of Canterbury with a view to obtaining the appointment of Days of National Prayer. His Majesty, our honoured King, favoured the project and several of such days were held, some on a Sunday, others on a weekday. The Sunday services were largely attended in the churches, and on the weekdays short but impressive periods of prayer were arranged in factories and places of public resort. At the close of the war, services of thanksgiving and praise were held throughout the land, in many of which a special form of worship issued by the Alliance, was used.

4. *Whitsuntide Calls to Prayer*. For many years the Council of the Alliance has sent out, in preparation for Whitsuntide, a letter appealing for special prayer that God would grant a new work of His Holy Spirit in Church and nation. This Call, approved by the Archbishops, has been signed by Bishops of the Church of England, heads of the Free Church denominations, leaders of Missionary Societies and representative laymen. Who can tell what has been the result in the spiritual realm of the sermons, addresses and concerts of prayer called forth?

5. *Prayer in the Home*. Side by side with its encouragement of public prayer, the Alliance has all along laid emphasis on the importance and value of Family Prayer. Large meetings to promote it have been held from time to time; a typical one having been that in the Queen's Hall, at which the Archbishop of Canterbury (Dr. Davidson) presided and among other

speakers were Bishop Taylor-Smith, Lord Kinnaird, Sir J. Compton-Rickett and the General Secretary.

The Alliance gave publicity to the words of Field-Marshal Earl Roberts on the subject. Shortly before his death, when writing to Lord Curzon, he said, "We have had family prayers for fifty-five years. One chief reason is that they bring the household together in a way that nothing else can. Then it ensures the servants and others who may be in the house joining in prayers which, for one reason or another, they may have omitted saying by themselves. We have never given any order about prayers: attendance is quite optional, but, as a rule, all the servants, men and women, come regularly on hearing the bell ring".

The influence of Family Prayer on the children of a home was tellingly shown by Dr. Stanford, of Denmark Place, Camberwell, in an address delivered during the Universal Week of Prayer. "What can we do," he asked, "for the dear ones who are so soon to take our place in the world? . . . Let us pray that we may pray aright, and that while we offer the right prayer in the right way, we may use the right means. Whatever means you use, whatever prayers you offer, there is no time to be lost. . . . While you are dreaming, that little girl is gone into a woman, that little boy is gone into a man; gone as the blossom is gone into the fruit, gone as the dawn is gone into the day!"

To help in the conduct of Family Prayer, the Executive of the Alliance issued a Prayer Card with petitions suited to the various events of home life. This was widely circulated, and in some places was distributed from house to house.

CHAPTER VI

THE PROCLAMATION OF THE GOSPEL

FROM its beginning the Alliance has stood as a lighthouse flashing out the glory of the Gospel. Its name "Evangelical" marks it out as a witness to the Evangel. The salient points of that great message were outlined in 1846 by the Rev. E. Bickersteth: "The incarnation of the Son of God: His work of atonement for us sinners – a finished work, His mediatorial intercession for which He ever lives, His supreme sovereignty and reign." And he adds, "The justification of the sinner by faith alone is the ground of a sinner's hope of righteousness before God. . . . It is the beginning of all true and solid peace in the soul, and of all delightful communion with God . . . and of all holy love to man".

To unite in making known this great Gospel and through it to bring men and women to God has all along been the practical object of the Alliance.

In 1856 an Honorary Secretary of the Alliance, Dr. Steane, called upon its members to join in special services for the evangelisation of the non-churchgoing masses. He told of the services which had been fostered by the Alliance in London the winter before. For three months every Sunday evening services had been held in Exeter Hall. Every one had been so largely attended that hundreds had gone away unable to get into the hall, and it was estimated that two-thirds of them were people not accustomed to go to any place of worship. Dr. Steane called for such united efforts wherever they could be made, and Evangelistic gatherings followed with hallowed results in many parts of the land.

When the American Evangelists, Moody and Sankey, came to England, the Alliance gave them warm support, chronicling their missions in its magazine. In London the Evangelists met a gathering of clergy and ministers in Freemasons' Hall, the birthplace of the Alliance, and a new and passionate impulse was imparted to the soul-winning endeavour of the Alliance.

No Evangelistic ministry in London has had a greater success than that of C. H. Spurgeon, and when, toward the end of it, he was asked what he would advise as likely to promote permanent union in truth, love and good works, he replied: "Let the Union have a simple basis of Bible truths.... I know of no better summary of these than that adopted by the Evangelical Alliance." So the beliefs which inspired Spurgeon in the building up of what was probably at that time the largest existing church were those which the Alliance was seeking to spread throughout the world.

The spirit of the Alliance in this respect was shown in the help given to the "Alliance Bible School", founded in Berlin for the Evangelisation of Europe. Pastor Warns, one of the Principals of the school, in acknowledging support, reports on bis journey to Austria, Hungary and Rumania. "It was indeed a real Alliance journey", he writes. "So varied were the bodies I was privileged to visit.... It is borne in upon our minds that the Bible School has a mission to these forgotten [sic] countries in South-East Europe." This work was carried out in face of much opposition.

RUSSIA

No land presents a sharper challenge to the Gospel than does Russia – Russia with its vast area, its great population, its spirit of religious desire, but its opposing rulers. Here the Alliance carried on work for many years, first through J. D. Kilburn and F. W. Baedeker, who journeyed through Russia, preaching the Gospel in prisons and distributing copies of the Scripture on river-boats and wherever they could find opportunity. Dr. Baedeker remarked in 1892 that prison doors were still open and in the prisons he had found "more liberty to preach the Gospel than outside". Dr. Baedeker has been styled "The Apostle of Russian Prisons".

These devoted pioneers were in time succeeded by Adam Podin, a big, manly Estonian, who represented the Alliance in Russia for many years. In those days the way was comparatively open and he went through all Russia, European and Asiatic, visiting the prisons. Coming to a gaol, he would interview the Governor and, having obtained permission, would go in, give Scriptures to the prisoners and preach to them of the love that redeems. He has told of his congregations of convicts, manacled hand and foot, and of the welcome they have given to the Saviour's story.

In Riga, Podin was warned not to make any effort to approach the prisoners, who were known for their wild and dangerous character. Two hundred of them were paraded in charge of soldiers with fixed bayonets and loaded rifles. The message of the visitor was that none were so sinful or so far from God that they could not be saved; and one is sure that that message was pressed home with a loving appeal. At the close one of the prisoners rushed to Podin, an officer following, thinking the man intended harm. But this was not so. The prisoner wanted to make sure that what he had just heard was true. On being assured that this was the case, he was satisfied and the prisoners spread out the Gospels they had received and began to study them. Similar experiences were encountered in Moscow, where 6,000 prisoners heard the Gospel, and in Reval and other cities. Again and again Podin had the solemn opportunity of speaking to men under sentence of death.

An important branch of the Alliance's Russian work was the Volga River Mission. The Volga, with its tributaries, waters an expanse greater than Britain, France and Germany combined, and on its banks are many of the great cities of Russia. It is 2,325 miles long, and in some places, and at some seasons, forty miles broad. The traffic on this mighty river gave a wonderful opportunity for the distribution of Scriptures, and for talks with men and women on the boats and at the quays. In such work the seed of the Kingdom was broadcast far and wide, and surely it is not lost, though the harvest cannot yet be seen.

ESTONIA

When Russia became closed to the propagation of the Gospel, Podin's work was continued in Estonia, and here he visited both prisons and leper asylums. One of his letters tells of both these kinds of work. Arriving in a town, he arranged for services in the prison and, by telephone, in the leper asylum. Soon he saw before him a congregation of convicts, warders and other officials. "After hymn and prayer", he writes, "I had for my text Luke xv. 1–10: Lost and found treasures." He spoke that day of the great love of the Good Shepherd who goes out to win the straying sheep, "so that He can bring him back to joy, peace and security for ever". "When I asked, 'Is there anyone who would like to have a resting place on the shoulder of that Good Shepherd who has carried me already thirty-four long years?' many burst out in tears, some grasping my hands (which is not allowed), trying to kiss them. . . . Many confessed Jesus as their Saviour."

"Next morning, very early", the letter continues, "I started with horse sledges in bitter cold weather to drive the twenty miles to my lepers. I arrived safely after several hours' drive." On entering the leper asylum he found the gangway and staircase decorated, as also were the church, altar-rail and pulpit from which he was to preach. The lepers were waiting for him. When he saw them in the midst of the decorations they had put up with their poor, mutilated hands "in a short time", he writes, "and out of pure love to me, I could not speak with dry eyes. It was more than I could bear. I preached the full salvation through Jesus and urged them to trust Jesus and take Him. After the service several confessed Christ as their Saviour, and when I left the church several were standing at the staircase begging for baptism. After this I visited some that were too sick to be brought into the church. Oh, it is glorious to be a comforter of such".

Podin carried on this Christlike ministry until the recent war made it impossible; and during that war he died. The Alliance has done no more beautiful work in her century of life than that which she did through Adam Podin.

POLAND

The Alliance has for several years worked in Poland through its Polish branch. In Warsaw, Lodz, Cracow and other cities, as well as in villages, the Gospel has been preached, and often to great congregations. The ministry of women, too, was fostered through the Deaconesses' "Motherhouse" at Wiecbork and the hospital at Thorn. Thus the Alliance has been the link between various centres of evangelism and mercy.

In 1937 a step forward was taken in the founding of a Bible School by the Alliance in co-operation with the representatives of several Churches and missions. The object of this was to train ministers and evangelists for work throughout Poland.

During the recent war such work has inevitably been greatly hindered and the Evangelicals, with the entire Polish nation, have suffered intensely; yet now, with ranks thinned indeed, but with spirit chastened and refined, they represent a hopeful Evangelical element in this new and difficult era in Eastern Europe.

MALTA

From the broad expanses of Russia and Poland we turn to the little island of Malta – small indeed geographically, but from the national standpoint the key to the Mediterranean and interesting to the Christian from its associations with the Apostle Paul. Here the Roman Catholic Church holds relentless sway, but the Evangelical Alliance saw in Malta a fortress that should be won and appointed to it its first native colporteur. God blessed his work and, in spite of opposition, a Maltese Evangelical Church was formed, with a minister belonging to the island.

The work in Malta was followed up by a mission to the Maltese in North Africa.

SPAIN

The work of the Alliance in Spain, carried on through its Spanish branch, has long been led by Don Fernando Cabrera, and evidence of its success was given in 1925, when a deputation from the British Executive visited a number of Spanish cities. In the Church of the Redeemer, Madrid, a Welcome Meeting was held, and the building was crowded, the chancel being filled with representatives of the Spanish Committee of the Alliance, said to include all Evangelical interests in the capital. Inspiring addresses were delivered, and a spirit of joy and enthusiasm prevailed.

The evident success of the work, however, has naturally varied with the degree of religious liberty granted by successive

Governments, and not long ago Roman Catholic influence caused the closing of most of the Protestant places of worship, while some of the ministers were imprisoned. Yet the work went on in quiet ways and there were conversions in prison.

Still more recently there has been some slackening of the restrictive policy, and reports tell of Evangelical services, including baptisms.

PORTUGAL

The Alliance has worked in Portugal many years. At the Diamond Jubilee Conference of the Alliance, in 1906, interesting testimony to it was borne by the Rev. R. H. Moreton, of Portugal. He told how at one time Evangelical work had come under a dark cloud, as the Prime Minister had ordered that all Protestant work in Lisbon should cease – "But presently," he added, "the Evangelical Alliance came in, and the cloud lifted." He went on to tell of the varied work which had grown up – Sunday Schools, Christian Endeavour Societies, Y.M.C.A., Y.W.C.A. – and Gospel services, not indeed in the open air, but permitted in buildings. A feature of the work had been the reaching of University students.

In recent years the Alliance, led by its Portuguese President, Senhor Eduardo Moreira, has worked jointly with the International Missionary Council in aiding the many missionaries who pass through Lisbon on their way to and from their spheres of service, in West Africa or South America. It is interesting to note that the Portuguese Evangelical Alliance has lately been domiciled in a former Marianos convent, in Lisbon. In this building inspiring services have been held, in which the glorious message of salvation through Christ alone has been sounded forth.

Senhor Moreira mentions that, whereas the great doctrines of Reformed Christianity had not been "defined" in Portuguese, they are now being given forth in a new encyclopaedia: also that the paper *Diario Popular*, in an article on Field-Marshal Montgomery, told of his reading the Bible every day and of his recommendation that the officers and men of his army should do the same. Senhor Moreira says that this aroused in Lisbon a noticeable interest in the Bible. So it is clear that in spite of hindrances the light breaks in.

GREECE

For years the Alliance has rejoiced to give help to the Greek Evangelical Church in its Gospel work in that classic but sorrowful land. In course of time twelve churches have been organised there, thousands of copies of the Bible in modern Greek have been circulated, and a recent witness tells that in every village there are those who echo the words of the Greeks who said to Philip, "Sir, we would see Jesus".

THE WEEK OF WITNESS

As an example of the general encouragement given to Evangelisation by the Alliance, mention may be made of Whitsuntide, 1923, when the Executive arranged a "Week of Witness". An appeal, translated into foreign languages, was issued, and the Week was observed in many lands. Exchanges of pulpit, night by night, testified to the unity of the effort and Evangelistic messages were delivered both on the mission field and at home. Inspiration was also given to Personal Evangelism, with the ideal of every Christian the winner of someone to Christ.

THE BRITISH EMPIRE BUNGALOW

In 1924 the British Empire Exhibition, held at Wembley, gave the Alliance a special opportunity, and a bungalow was erected in "Quality Street", for the reception of visitors and the holding of prayer services and conversations on spiritual matters. The bungalow was a pleasant and attractive little building, with the Alliance motto, "Unum Corpus Sumus in Christo", set out in clear lettering along the roof; and in it, in the very heart of the Exhibition, people from many lands were able to find rest, friendship and a "season of refreshing".

In addition to this, the Alliance joined with other Christian bodies in securing the large Conference Hall of the Exhibition for Evangelistic addresses by John McNeill and Gipsy Smith.

The next year, as the Exhibition was continued, the bungalow was again utilised, and a special effort was made to influence the numerous workers engaged in the Exhibition.

MANIFESTO ON EVANGELISM

A recent act of the Alliance Executive has been the issue of a manifesto calling attention to the critical character of our time, in which human plans which left God out of account have resulted in unutterable ruin. It is urged that the Voice of God is sounding amid the dread events of the war and its sequel, and is calling men to return to Him.

The way of return is shown to be by Jesus Christ, who gave Himself to redeem men from their sins, and earnest appeal is made to the followers of Christ to renew their endeavours, in reliance on the power of the divine Spirit, to win the people to God.

400th Anniversary of the Augsburg Confession
The General Secretary (Mr. H. M. Gooch) addressing
the representatives of the United Nations (see page 56)

International Protestant League Conference Group at Podebrady, Czechoslovakia (see page 56)

British Empire Exhibition, 1925-26
Christian Service Bungalow   Front view

Back view of the Bungalow (see page 47)

*Prayer Book Revision
The Royal Albert Hall Meeting
arranged by the Alliance, 1925
(see page 55)*

CHAPTER VII

PROTESTANT WITNESS

BECAUSE the Alliance exists to promote the unity of Evangelical believers, it has from the beginning resisted the teaching and practices of the Roman Catholic Church, which in so many ways obscures the light of the New Testament and leads into paths of error. The Evangelical Alliance rejects the priesthood, culminating in the Papacy, which comes between the individual Christian and the Lord; the exaltation of the Mother of Jesus to a place as Queen of Heaven, which our Lord never gave her; the denial of the right of private judgment on the Christian's part and claim for his acceptance of the authority of the Church; the withholding of the Bible from the common people; the teaching of Baptismal Regeneration and that the bread and wine in the "Mass" become the body and blood of Christ.

The Evangelical Alliance stands for the sole Saviourhood of Christ; the salvation of the sinner through faith in Him who died for us; the privilege of every believer to come directly by Christ to God, without the intervention of any human priest, and his right to believe and act according to conscience, enlightened by the teaching of the New Testament.

At the formation of the Alliance one of its objects was declared to be the resistance of Popery, and the Alliance was still young when in March, 1851, its Glasgow Committee resolved to offer prizes for the best essays against Romanism. The first prize was won by the Rev. J. A. Wylie, of Edinburgh, with an essay entitled The Papacy. In this valuable book the author traced the origin of the Papacy in the period when early Christianity lost its glowing life and when old idolatries – Magian, Greek, Roman – united under a Christian form; he showed the uprise of the Temporal Sovereignty, the false dogmas of the Papacy and its evil influence on the history of nations.

Mr. Wylie's book is still useful as a clear and well-reasoned statement of the Protestant case against Rome.

DOGMA OF THE IMMACULATE CONCEPTION

The ink can hardly have been dry on Mr. Wylie's book when the Pope added a new dogma to those taught by Rome. This was the Dogma of the Immaculate Conception, according to which the Virgin Mary was conceived without taint of sin. It was a part of the Romish glorification of Mary, and has no foundation in the New Testament.

Some of the Roman Catholic Bishops received it with enthusiasm, declaring that the declaration of the dogma would bring unspeakable blessing to believers; others were neutral; many opposed.

THE ABBE LABORDE

Among those who opposed was the Abbe Laborde, priest at Lectoure, in France. M. Laborde wrote a pamphlet against the dogma, for which he was reprimanded by his Archbishop. He was, however, a strong man and had the courage to go to Rome, to appeal to the Pope. There he offered to sustain in public debate the following thesis: "The doctrine of the Immaculate Conception is a new opinion in the Church; it is not contained in the Scriptures, and has not come from the Apostles by the channel of tradition." The Pope refused his request, and ordered him to leave Rome. When he did not do so he was summoned before the tribunal of the Inquisition, who repeated the order of the Pope. Next day the constables of the Government invaded his lodgings, laid hands upon him and conveyed him to a ship sailing for France.

The Evangelical Alliance published a caustic account of the affair, showing that Popery had shown once more that liberty of thought and discussion is absolutely repugnant to it.

THE "MIRACLE" OF LA SALETTE

In 1852 the Roman Catholic world was thrilled by an announcement that the Virgin Mary had appeared on the mountain of La Salette, near Grenoble. Two children, a boy of twelve and a girl of ten, stated that she had appeared to them in the form of a beautiful woman with a floating scarf and a blue robe, and had spoken to them in the patois of their country. This extravagant tale was eagerly caught up for the purposes of Rome. The water of a fountain which flows on the mountain was sold in bottles and brought in, it was said, a return of 150,000 francs. The Bishop of the diocese, with numerous clergy, repaired to the spot and there laid the first stone of a chapel, to be erected to "Notre Dame de la Salette".

The attitude of the Evangelical Alliance to all this was shown in the exposure of it in an article in *Evangelical Christendom*, emanating from the French branch of the Alliance.

INFALLIBILITY OF THE POPE

In 1870 the Roman Catholic Bishops, brought together from all over the world, discussed at great length, and finally passed, a declaration that the Pope is the only, and infallible, medium of communication between Heaven and earth; that speaking in his capacity as Pope, and without other human counsel, he is invested by God with authority to determine infallibly all questions of faith and morals. Later on came the proclamation of this dogma in the Council Hall of St. Peter's Cathedral, Rome. The Roll of Bishops was there called, and 533 replied *"Placet"*, and only two *"Non placet"*; one from Southern Italy, the other from America. The spectators shouted *"Viva il Papa Infallibile."* And so this dogma in which the attributes of God are claimed for a man became a part of the doctrine of the Roman Church.

The Evangelical Alliance denounced it at the time in its *Chronicle of the Churches*, saying that in answer to the questions of thoughtful men perplexed with doubts Rome's reply was, "Hush your doubts, perplexities and unbeliefs: I have the secret of truth. Listen to me and live: refuse me and perish."

It is reassuring to know that this dogma was not received without protest by Roman Catholics. Many of the Bishops left Rome before the deciding vote; and after the vote had fixed the position many leaders declined to accept it. Opposition was specially strong in Southern Germany, being led by Dr. Dollinger, of Munich. Dollinger and his party went so far as to form an independent body, which became known as the "Old Catholic Church" and spread to other countries, notably to Switzerland and Austria.

INSPECTION OF CONVENTS

In this same year the Alliance gave its support to a movement for the inspection of nunneries. The matter arose in Parliament, where attention was called to the thousands of English women who, voluntarily or not, were shut up in institutions in which the law could exert no power, either to redress, or to prevent, wrong. The motion was carried in the House of Commons by a small majority, but every effort was made by Roman Catholics to prevent action being taken. The cry of persecution was raised, and this important issue was shelved.

GLADSTONE AND THE VATICAN DECREES

In 1874 the Alliance welcomed the action of W. E. Gladstone in publishing a pamphlet on the *Vatican Decrees*, in which be declared in regard to Rome that since the promulgation of the decrees of 1870, declaring the Pope's Infallibility, and claiming for his commands an absolute and unquestioning obedience from all Christians, "no man could become her convert without renouncing his moral and mental freedom, and placing his civil loyalty and duty at the mercy of another". The organ of the Alliance warmly supported Mr. Gladstone.

THE CONFESSIONAL

In 1877 the publication of a book entitled *The Priest in Absolution*, by the Anglican Society of the Holy Cross, led to a widespread outburst of opposition to the Confessional, especially the Confessional in the English Church. Protest was made by a great meeting at Exeter Hall and in the organ of the Alliance. Appeal against the introduction of auricular confession was made to the Archbishops and Bishops of the Church of England by ninety-six members of the peerage. This appeal met with a sympathetic response, and as the outcome of continued discussion the Society of the Holy Cross agreed to supply no further copies of the book which had caused alarm. The Confessional, however, continues among us.

LOS VON ROM

Early in the present century an appeal for help came to the British Committee of the Evangelical Alliance from the "Los von Rom" movement in Central Europe. This movement arose in Bohemia, one of the first battle-grounds of the Reformation, where John Hus, a disciple of Wycliffe, preached till the Roman Catholics burned him in 1415. In the Hussite wars which followed, the Reformed party were defeated and Bohemia was left at the mercy of Ferdinand II, a disciple of the Jesuits. A cruel persecution ensued, in which the chiefs of the nobles were executed and the people hunted with dogs. The result was the suppression of the Reformation there, and Bohemia became a Roman Catholic country.

With the passing of centuries, however, the spirit of faith and independence re-awoke and a cry for freedom, both political and religious, arose. Taking as their watchword "Los von Rom", many came out from the Church of Rome.

A Committee was formed in Prague which organised Protestant churches, and soon there were more than ninety stations in Bohemia and Moravia, the work spreading quickly among the youth of the towns. At this stage financial need was felt, and it was now that the call for aid was addressed to the Evangelical Alliance. The Alliance gladly laid the appeal before the British public in 1903.

The work spread to other parts of Austria, and many thousands separated from Rome, some becoming members of the Lutheran Church, and others of the Reformed. In the year 1935 it was estimated that 302,571 were members of the Lutheran churches and 15,316 of the Reformed.

THE "NE TEMERE" DECREE

In 1911 the Alliance found it necessary to take strenuous action in opposition to a decree which had been issued by the Pope in 1909, This decree was named after its first two words –

"Ne Temere" – "Lest rashly"; the meaning being "Lest" anyone should get married "rashly", and not in accordance with the rules of the Roman Church. The decree laid down that "only those marriages are valid which are contracted before the parish priest". This meant that if a Roman Catholic married a Protestant and the marriage was conducted by a Protestant minister, that marriage was null and void, and any children resulting from it were illegitimate. Now the British State, like other Protestant States, regards marriage as a *civil* contract, no minister's presence being essential to its legality. The Pope's decree, reviving a regulation imposed by the Council of Trent in 1545, thus runs counter to British law and interferes with the liberty of British subjects – as with the subjects of other Protestant Governments.

The evil effects of this decree were brought to notice in 1911, through a scandalous case which arose in Belfast. Three years before, a Presbyterian girl had been married by her own minister to a Roman Catholic. Apparently the marriage proved happy until a Romish priest told the husband of the "Ne Temere" decree and insisted that he was living in concubinage and his two little children were illegitimate. The result was the breaking up of the home and the loss by the wife of her husband, her children, and even her clothing, except what she was wearing.

The case caused great indignation and the Evangelical Alliance called two public meetings of protest, the first at the Church House, Westminster, the second at the Queen's Hall. The Queen's Hall meeting is said to have been attended by some 3,000 persons, an overflow meeting having to be held in a smaller hall. Lord Kinnaird presided and addresses of passionate protest were delivered by several speakers, including the Rev. W. Corkey, of Belfast, the Rev. Dinsdale T. Young, the Right Honourable J. H. Campbell, M.P. for Dublin University, and Dr. John Clifford. Resolutions denouncing the "Ne Temere" decree were unanimously passed.

It is disappointing to reflect that this infamous decree is still in force and is causing distress in different parts of the British Empire, especially in Malta, where the grip of the Romish Church is so strong and so severe.

THE REVISION OF THE PRAYER BOOK

In 1923 British Christianity was deeply exercised upon the question of Prayer Book revision.

The proposals for revision arose from two motives; one, the desire to bring the services of the Church of England into closer accord with modern needs; the other, the wish to meet the views of Anglo-Catholics and so to make them more happy in the Church of which they are members. Evangelicals, within and outside the Anglican Church, opposed the revision on the ground that it tended to weaken the Protestant character of the Church, drawing it nearer to Rome and farther from the Evangelical Free Churches. It was felt that the changes proposed would restore elements which in the Reformation were definitely rejected, and would tend in the direction of the Mass and of the Adoration of the Sacramental Bread, regarded as transformed into the Body of Christ.

The Evangelical Alliance entered with all its heart into the resistance offered to the revision. A meeting was called to emphasise "The Message of the Reformation for Today". This was held at the Queen's Hall, and the hall was crowded with an assembly enthusiastic in its support of Reformation principles.

THE MALINES CONVERSATIONS

At that time the urgency of the position was underlined by the Malines Conversations, in which a party of Anglo-Catholics, led by Lord Halifax, conferred in the Belgian city with a group of Romanists led by Cardinal Mercier, as to the differences, and possible agreement, between the Roman and Anglican Churches. The conversations yielded little result, except to show once more the adherence of Rome to Papal Infallibility and the system associated with it.

PRAYER BOOK REVISION AGAIN

Next year, 1925, as the Prayer Book conflict was still going on, the Evangelical Alliance held a great gathering in the Royal Albert Hall, London, in resistance to the revision –

and another in 1926. At these meetings the utmost unity and earnestness prevailed in the witness of both speakers and hearers to the determination of British Protestants to preserve undimmed the glory of their faith. The Revised Prayer Book was rejected by Parliament, and the later one, suggested by the Bishops, met with a similar fate in 1928. So it was made clear that Britain is still a Protestant country, and the Church of England a Protestant Church.

THE AUGSBURG CONFESSION

In June, 1930, a celebration took place in Augsburg (Bavaria) of the 40th anniversary of the Augsburg Confession – drawn up in that city in 1530 by the German Diet, under the leadership of the Reformer Melanchthon (Luther being then under the ban of the Emperor). In this Confession the Protestant leaders stated, first, their points of agreement with Rome, and then their points of difference.

The Council of the Evangelical Alliance presented an address of congratulation to the Augsburg assembly, expressing their joy in the historic Confession of Faith which first set out the great Protestant doctrines in clear language which all might understand. They commissioned their secretary, Mr. H. Martyn Gooch, to represent them at the celebration. This he did, speaking at the great gathering in the Barfusser Church as a representative of Protestant churches in Europe and America.

INTERNATIONAL PROTESTANT LEAGUE

In view of the renewed activity of the Roman Catholic Church in every sphere of life, a new League was formed on the Continent for the Defence and Furtherance of Protestantism. The President and Secretary of this League visited London in 1931, and were welcomed to the Annual Meetings of the Alliance. At these they gave encouraging reports of the movement, which had now spread to nearly every European country, as well as to America and South Africa.

CATHOLIC ACTION

In recent years the attention of the Alliance has been given to the movement known as "Catholic Action", called for by Pope Pius XI, and carried into effect in many lands throughout the world. Its purpose is to secure the active co-operation of Roman Catholic laymen in bringing influence to bear on public affairs. In a pastoral letter a Roman Catholic Archbishop defined its objects as including the defence of faith and morals, "justice for our schools", the promotion and protection of the rights and interests of Catholics, circulating Catholic literature in public libraries, watching the public Press in order to challenge "misstatements", correction of "false history" in school-books, and the "adequate representation" of Catholics in Parliament and other public bodies.

At a Congress of the International Protestant League held in Holland, Mr. Gooch, the Alliance Secretary, detailed the forms already taken by Catholic Action in many lands, strengthening the hold of Rome upon the schools, the Press and the public life of nations, and he urged that Protestants should unite more closely in resistance to them. As a practical point he suggested that Protestants should refrain from sending their children, especially the girls, to convent schools.

CHAPTER VIII

RELIGIOUS LIBERTY AND SUCCOUR OF THE PERSECUTED

ONE of the chief objects of the Alliance throughout its hundred years' history has been the vindication of religious liberty, the right of every man to hear the Voice of God for himself and to obey the divine command which comes to him. The Alliance denies the right of any man, or authority to come between the soul and its Maker. And where spiritual freedom is denied and men and women are punished for seeking to exercise it, the Alliance counts it its duty, and privilege, to go to the succour of the persecuted. So for a century the Alliance has sought to be a champion of those who suffer for Christ and conscience.

THE CANTON DE VAUD

In 1846, the year of the birth of the Alliance, a religious crisis arose in the Canton de Vaud, in Switzerland. Here a Free Church denomination was organised on a scale which was felt to be new in French-speaking countries. It was met with determined opposition by the Council of State of the canton. The first step of the Council in suppression of this Free Church was taken in the passing of a law which enacted that every man engaged in public instruction, "from the first professor down to the lowest schoolmaster", who should attend any religious service out of the "official" Church should be liable to dismissal from his office. This law was put into execution immediately, and applied to the first educational body in the canton – the Academy of Lausanne. All the professorships were declared vacant, including that of the famous Professor Vinet.

A Free Academy was formed, which was joined by nearly thirty of the theological students of the "official" academy, and the work of organising the new Church continued. Services were held in many private houses and, the movement being seen to be in harmony with the principles of the Evangelical Alliance, the British Committee of the Alliance invited special weekly prayer for the brethren in Lausanne and other parts of Switzerland, to whom religious liberty was being denied.

The persecution, however, continued and a decree was published in the Canton de Vaud forbidding the holding of *any* assemblies for religious purposes except those of the churches of the Government. By this decree nearly 6,000 persons were deprived of the public means of grace. Meetings were still held in private houses, but there were dangers as the police and armed soldiers paraded the streets to discover unlawful assemblies and some shots were fired.

The British section of the Alliance held meetings of protest and from Glasgow a memorial was adopted for transmission to the Council of State. This body, however, carried forward its policy by arresting, fining and expelling Free Church ministers. In spite of this the Free churches continued to grow in strength. In the absence of ministers, services were conducted by elders, and some gatherings were held in secluded spots on the Swiss mountains.

In the midst of these events an informal branch of the Evangelical Alliance was formed, though it was impossible to hold a public meeting in the canton. After a long time of trial the spirit of intolerance died down among the rulers of the canton and liberty of worship came to the Free churches.

It was like the story of England in Charles II's reign.

ROME

In 1849 the case of Dr. Achilli caused the leaders of the Alliance much anxiety. Formerly a Romanist priest in high standing, he had become a Protestant and had circulated the Bible in Rome. He had been arrested and was imprisoned in the Castle of St. Angelo, from which he was to be transferred to the prison of the Inquisition. Moral charges were trumped up against him and his life was in imminent danger.

The British organisation of the Alliance appointed a deputation, including Sir Culling Eardley, Baptist Noel and

Dr. Steane, to go to Paris and appeal for justice to the French Government, as Rome was at that time occupied by France. If necessary, they were to go on to Rome. In the meantime it was decided to hold a "Special Meeting for United Prayer" that God would preserve the deputation in their journey and grant success to their mission. The meeting was called for eight o'clock one morning at Carr's Lane Chapel Vestry, Birmingham. Breakfast was to be provided, when the circumstances of Dr. Achilli's case would be explained by the Rev. J. Angell James and Dr. Nelson. A season of prayer was to follow, closing at ten o'clock.

The letter calling this prayer meeting is before me as I write. The paper on which it is printed is discoloured with time and the notes written upon it are in the handwriting of long ago, but it is a document of living interest, speaking of the faith in God, and the sympathy with His suffering servants, of the men who founded the Alliance.

The deputation went to Paris and was favourably received by the Foreign Minister, M. de Tocqueville, who sent instructions to Rome that Dr. Achilli was not to be transferred to the Inquisition. Ultimately Dr. Achilli was released and came to this country, where he was welcomed with honour by the Executive of the Alliance and by a public meeting called by them in Exeter Hall. Later, he was received at large gatherings in English, Scottish and Irish cities.

SWEDEN: PERSECUTION OF PROTESTANTS BY PROTESTANTS

Early in 1850 it became known that a Baptist minister, Frederick Nilsson, was being persecuted on the instigation of Lutheran clergy. Nilsson had long been a Baptist and now had accepted the pastorate of a small Baptist church in Gothenburg. This brought him under the law of the criminal code, and, although a man of godly life and character, he was tried and sentenced to perpetual banishment, with confiscation of his property.

The Alliance Executive drew up a memorial, appealing on Nilsson's behalf to the King of Sweden, to be transmitted through the Swedish Ambassador, a copy of it being forwarded to Lord Palmerston.

Nilsson appealed against his sentence and, while the verdict of the Supreme Court was awaited, the Lutheran clergy of the neighbourhood from which his congregation was drawn visited the members of Nilsson's church and threatened them with similar legal proceedings unless they returned to the Lutheran Church. Nilsson obtained an interview with the King, who received him kindly, but the Supreme Court confirmed the sentence and so strong was the insistence of the Lutheran leaders that the King felt unable to cancel the sentence. This good man was therefore exiled and his flock dispersed. The Alliance had done what it could for him, but the case reminds us that success is not always granted to human endeavour. God has His plans, and they are sometimes fulfilled through the continued trial of His people. Yet this does not exonerate those who treat them unjustly.

TUSCANY

In 1851 and following years a Romanist persecution of Protestants was carried on by the Duke of Tuscany at Florence. A decree was signed, authorising any magistrate to imprison any person known to possess or to read the Bible. Prominent among the sufferers under this decree was a member of the Florentine nobility, Count Guicciardini. He had renounced Romanism and was attending Protestant worship. Sleeplessly watched by the Jesuits, he was purposing to leave for England, to attend the Conference of the Evangelical Alliance. This seems to have become known and he was arrested and imprisoned.

The Committee of the Alliance at once took steps on his behalf; Sir Culling Eardley, Dr. Steane and others interviewing British statesmen who promised to use their friendly offices on the Count's behalf.

THE MADIAI

Other arrests followed in Florence; among them that of Dr. Geymonat, in later years the President of the Waldensian College in that city: but the case which has excited most general interest is that of the Madiai, husband and wife.

Francesco and Rosa Madiai were arrested on suspicion of heresy. In the examination which followed, they avowed themselves Protestants and were remanded to separate cells.

In this persecution the special efforts to stop the reading of the Bible suggest that a desire for the sacred Word prevailed in Florence, and this was the case. As people were no longer able to meet in public places to read the Scripture together, they would do it secretly in by-streets of the city or out in the fields and along the banks of the river. Some persons copied in manuscript the greater part of the New Testament from one which had been lent them to read.

The two Madiai were kept under conditions which severely tried their health. At length came their trial. What was their fault? That they had read the Bible and sought to live in accordance with its teaching. Francesco was asked whether he was born in the Roman Catholic Church? "Yes," he answered, "but now I am a Christian according to the Gospel." They were sentenced – Francesco to fifty-six months of the galleys with hard labour, and Rosa to forty-four months in the female galleys, also with hard labour.

After the trial, Rosa wrote from her cell a letter to her husband, in which she said: "I have always loved you, but how much more ought I to love you now that we have been together in the battle of the Great King – that we have been beaten, but not vanquished! I hope that through the merits of Jesus Christ, God, our Father, will have accepted our testimony. My good Madiai, life is only a day and a day of grief! Yesterday we were young, today we are old! Nevertheless we can say with old Simeon 'Lord, now lettest Thou Thy servant depart in peace, for mine eyes have seen Thy Salvation.'"

The Committee of the Alliance passed resolutions expressive of its indignation at the cruel treatment of these innocent God-fearing people-these resolutions to be published in *The Times*. A deputation interviewed Lord John Russell, the Secretary for Foreign Affairs, and a large meeting of protest was held in Exeter Hall. Then a deputation was sent to Florence to plead with the Duke, and on Friday evening, March 18th, 1853, Lord John Russell announced in the House of Commons that a telegram had that day been received, conveying the news that the Madiai were liberated. They had been released as secretly as possible to avoid public demonstrations in their favour. They went to the South of France for rest, and thirteen years afterwards it was written: "The Madiai are avenged! A few short years have glided away, and Florence has become the headquarters of the Waldensian Church."

SAXE MEININGEN

In the early eighteen-fifties religious liberty was being infringed in several of the German States, among them Saxe Meiningen. Here the Baptists were the special objects of repression. A Government decree prohibited their meetings and the observance of the Lord's Supper; the pastor was interdicted from visiting his people, and anyone who received him into his house was liable to a penalty.

Yet the members of the little Church managed to meet in secret. On one occasion they even held a baptism, though the pastor narrowly escaped capture by the police.

Another time they held the Lord's Supper in the depths of a pine forest. "Our table," said one of them, "was the mossy turf. I spread that table with a white cloth. How beautiful did the cup of the Lord appear upon it, while a few stars looked down from a clouded sky! It was so dark in the gloom of the forest that we could scarcely see the bread. But our hearts were the more full of joy as we had so long missed this sacred privilege. In the commemoration of our Lord's death He had strengthened our faith and love, and we joined in a song in the loneliness of a night in the forest."

Appeal was made on behalf of these persecuted Christians to the Minister of the Interior at the Ducal Palace. He was asked whether these Baptists were politically, or otherwise than religiously, troublesome. He replied, "Not at all!" He believed them to be very good people, except that they would hold their own views on religious subjects, and act upon them.

The Evangelical Alliance published these facts and a little later appealed to the King of Prussia to use his influence to secure religious liberty in the German States. This he evidently did and in the course of time the restrictions were annulled.

VARIOUS GERMAN STATES

In October, 1855, a deputation of the Alliance, headed by Sir Culling Eardley, had an interview in Cologne with King Frederick William IV, of Prussia, respecting the persecution of "Dissenters" then taking place in various parts of Germany. In some of the States the rulers were avowing their hostility to the freedom of any religious community, except the Established Church, and marriage among "Dissenters" was being rendered impossible. In one place the Baptist minister was sent to prison for six months for daring to baptise, and in some instances whole congregations were sentenced to fourteen days' imprisonment for leaving the national Church.

The King received the information given with surprise and with sympathy, promising to do what he could to secure religious liberty in his own and the other States.

TURKEY

In 1855, as the outcome of the Alliance Conference held in Paris, an international group, headed by Sir Culling Eardley, sent a memorial to the Turkish Sultan, appealing to him against the Mohammedan custom of inflicting death on persons of their faith who change their creed.

A happy sequel resulted. In February, 1856, the Sultan issued to his Vizier a firman declaring freedom of religion to all his subjects. In this he said, "As all forms of religion are and shall be freely professed in my empire, no subject shall be hindered in the exercise of the religion he professes, nor shall be in any way annoyed on this account. Such being my wishes and my commands, you, who are my Grand Vizier, will, according to custom, cause this Imperial firman to be published in my capital, and in all parts of my empire."

It is, of course, true that in later years, and in special localities, Moslem intolerance has blazed forth and converts from Islam in Turkey have been ill-treated or even put to death, but it was a great thing to obtain from the ruler of the land a declaration of the principle of religious liberty and a prohibition of any act violating it.

The difficulty, however, of ensuring religious liberty in Turkey was illustrated twenty years later, when, in 1875, the Alliance, receiving renewed reports of the ill-treatment of Christians in that land, sent a deputation to Constantinople to interview the then reigning Sultan. On arrival they were refused access to him, but afterwards the Sultan gave an interview to the British Ambassador in which he informed him, in reference to the visit denied to the deputation, that "the late Grand Vizier had misunderstood his duty", as His Majesty would have been glad to receive them. So some time after the causes of complaint were removed and the British Executive sent the Sultan a letter thanking him for his interposition on behalf of the oppressed Christians.

SPAIN: THE MATAMOROS CASE

It was in the early eighteen-sixties that there occurred what is probably the most notable example of the Alliance action on behalf of the persecuted.

A young Spaniard, named Manuel Matamoros, was converted to Christ and to Protestantism. His home was in Malaga, in Southern Spain, and, being a man of decision and loyalty, he soon began to work for Christ in his own town. He succeeded in winning many to Evangelical belief and in training some to become preachers. The movement spread to Granada, Seville and even distant Barcelona. While he was in Barcelona he was arrested in consequence of a message sent from Granada, and brought before the magistrates. In his examination he was asked, "Do you profess the Catholic Apostolic Roman faith, and if not, what religion do you profess?" He replied, "My religion is that of Jesus Christ: my rule of faith is the Word of God, or Holy Bible. . . . The Roman Catholic and Apostolic Church not being based upon these principles, I do not believe in her dogmas, still less do I obey her in practice." The tribunal appeared astonished at these words, and the judge said to him, "Do you know what you are saying?" "Yes, sir," he replied. "I cannot deny it: I have put my hand to the plough, and I dare not look back." The judge was silent, and the tribunal rose.

Matamoros was now summoned to appear before the Council of Granada, where his work had been specially done.

This meant a journey on foot of 700 miles in the company of criminals. In the meantime, however, news of these proceedings had reached Paris and London, and money was sent to defray his travelling expenses to Malaga by sea, and thence by diligence to Granada.

In the diligence he met with the British statesman Sir Robert Peel, who was travelling with Lady Peel and her sister. Struck with the appearance of Matamoros, Sir Robert spoke to him, and afterwards, with the ladies, visited him in the dungeon in which he was confined. Sir Robert obtained for him some relaxation of the severity of his treatment and on his return to England spoke warmly on his behalf in the House of Commons.

The Evangelical Alliance Executive, deeply concerned, made representations to the Foreign Office and raised contributions towards the support of the families of Matamoros and some fellow-believers who were suffering with him.

In the prison at Granada the treatment of the prisoners became more cruel as months passed by. During the interval before the trial an insurrection broke out at Loja, between Granada and Malaga. This was purely political, but the enemies of the Protestant prisoners charged them with having instigated it. For this imputed crime they were prosecuted and false witnesses were suborned to give evidence against them. But at the last moment the plot fell through, as the man on whose testimony everything turned was stung by his guilty conscience and confessed all, giving an account of the bribes given to secure his false witness.

At length judgment on the original charge was pronounced on these sufferers for Christ. They had been acquitted of any political fault, but they were guilty of apostasy from the Romish Church and of propagating the faith they now loved. They received a cruel sentence – seven years' penal servitude, loss of civic rights and the payment of the cost of the prosecution. Against this sentence they appealed, but the public prosecutor also appealed, demanding its increased severity.

The case stood over till October, 1862, when Matamoros was sentenced to eight years' and his companion, Alhama, to nine years' penal servitude.

Both men appealed again and in April, 1863, both were condemned to penal servitude for nine years. During two and a half years these brave men had been kept in prison and subjected to great cruelty, but their faith had never wavered. The letters of Matamoros from prison are precious spiritual documents. In one he writes, "I have given myself entirely to God, through the most sweet name of Jesus. I am His. He will open the door of my prison, if He sees it meet for me and for all. . . . My end and aim is Jesus, and being so, ought I to shrink from, or refuse to bear, sorrow or persecution for His name's sake? No: for He sought out His sufferings for us. . . . The pathway to heaven is the pathway of the cross."

In the meanwhile the scope of the persecution was widening. The houses of respectable persons were being entered at midnight and their inmates carried off to prison. An English gentleman, writing from Spain in 1861, said, "There are now thirty-four Protestants in prison in various parts of Spain." (Twelve of these were liberated later.)

While all this was going on in Spain extraordinary things were taking place in other lands. The Evangelical Alliance's application to the British Foreign Office had met with sympathy, but Lord Russell, the Minister, feared the Spanish Government would resent any interference. The Spanish Ambassador had then been approached and the subject was repeatedly brought before the House of Commons, and by Sir Robert Peel, for the second time. Petitions then flowed into the House from Edinburgh, Glasgow, Liverpool and other places where the Alliance had committees, and it was again brought before Parliament by the Hon. Arthur Kinnaird. Lord Palmerston, in reply, promised that Her Majesty's Government would do anything it could to help.

These efforts in Parliament were supplemented by a great meeting in St. James's Hall, at which Lord Shaftesbury presided and Sir Robert Peel was the chief speaker.

It was at this time (1861) that the Geneva Conference of the Alliance was held. "Religious liberty" occupied one session, and a brilliant address upon it was delivered by Dr. de Pressensé. After dealing with general principles, the speaker turned to the Spanish prisoners and asked, "Shall we do nothing, gentlemen, for those glorious and well-beloved captives?" The Conference adopted a resolution expressing their "protest before Christian Europe against these persecutions", and committing to their various committees the taking of active measures. They also deputed two of their number to visit the prisoners and convey to them messages of Christian love, with a letter signed on behalf of the Conference.

Following upon the Conference, the British Committee of the Alliance deputed one of its members, General Alexander, to visit Madrid and lay the prisoners' case before the Duke of Tetuan, the Prime Minister of Spain. This he did but received no encouragement.

It was now felt that a more widely-representative approach must be made. A day of special prayer was observed in many lands and preparations were made for an international deputation to Madrid.

While this was taking place the Protestant ladies of France, to the number of about 30,000, signed a petition to Queen Isabella II, of Spain, and sent it by a deputation of their own. The petition was presented to the Queen by the Duke de Montpensier, but without success. The Queen is reported to have said that, had the prisoners been political offenders, or common criminals, she might have listened to the prayer of the petition, but that they were heretics, and this was a matter between her conscience and God; adding that she would rather have her right arm cut off than sign for them an act of grace.

The Alliance Committee, however, went on with their preparations, and a deputation was formed, including distinguished representatives from Austria, Bavaria, Denmark, France, Great Britain, Holland, Prussia, Sweden and Switzerland.

The deputation were in Madrid on Tuesday, May 19th, 1863, and met the next morning for mutual introduction and conference as to their mode of procedure. In the evening they assembled again: this time for the reading of the Scriptures and prayer. Earnest petitions ascended for the success of their mission, and on returning from this meeting Mr. Schmettau, the Secretary to the deputation, hearing an evening paper (La Correspondencia) cried in the streets, bought one and there read the announcement that the Government had commuted the sentence to as many years' banishment as the prisoners had been condemned to penal servitude.

The deputation prepared an address to the Queen of Spain, thanking her for the change in the sentence, but appealing still that the sentence should be remitted altogether. This, however, was not conceded and the prisoners were banished from their native land.

A copy of the letter to the Queen was sent to *The Times*, in which it appeared, in the original French with all the signatures, on June 3rd, 1863. Copies of it were taken by various members of the deputation, to be published in their own countries.

Matamoros, expelled from Spain, found a home, first at Pau, then at Bayonne, and, finally, at Lausanne, in Switzerland. Here he devoted himself to the training of young Spanish Protestants who wished to become preachers of the Gospel, and his Christ-like character and life won him abounding affection. His sufferings, however, had undermined his constitution and he died on July 31st, 1866, in his thirty-second year.

No longer an exile, he had passed while still young to the Homeland and the Father's House.

PERSIA: "WHERE IS THE EVANGELICAL ALLIANCE?"

The Nestorian Christians in Persia, numbering about 200,000 persons, had long been persecuted by the Mohammedans of that land, and at last resolved to appeal to the Evangelical Alliance for help. Two of them set out from Oroomiah in May, 1861. They travelled on foot through Armenia and Russia to Moscow (which took them six months), and from Moscow through Poland and Germany to Hamburg. Here they met with friends who placed them on board a steamer for London, where they arrived, having no language but their own. They had spent twelve months, including a hard winter, walking from Persia to Hamburg, and on reaching London they did not know where to turn. They managed, however, to pick up a few words of English and their first question was "Where is the Evangelical Alliance?"

They found it, received help, and were sent back to Persia with the promise that the Alliance would appeal to the Shah on behalf of the Nestorian Church.

A memorial was presented to the Shah and was graciously received. His Majesty dismissed the Moslem official who had oppressed the Nestorians and not only ordered the redress of their grievances but gave them land on which to build new churches in place of those destroyed, and £100 towards the cost of rebuilding. This royal gift was followed by further contributions from Persian officials and others.

When the Shah visited London shortly afterwards the Council of the Alliance approached him with a grateful acknowledgment of his help.

MADAGASCAR

In the mid-nineteenth century the Alliance recorded with sorrow the terrible persecution in Madagascar of Christians won from paganism by the devoted missionaries of the London Missionary Society. The Queen of Madagascar was the relentless enemy of the Christians, many of whom suffered death by poison, by burning, or by being hurled over a precipice.

It was with joy that in 1868 the Alliance in its organ announced the change of scene when a new Queen announced herself a Christian and set herself to promote the faith the earlier one bad tried to destroy. "What," she asked, "have I to do any more with idols? I trust in the true God."

RUSSIA

In 1871 the Alliance organised a memorable deputation, representing many nations, to lay before the Tsar, Alexander II, the wrongs of the Protestants in the Baltic Provinces. His Majesty was visiting the King and Queen of Wurttemberg at Friedrichshafen, on Lake Constance, and he appointed Prince Gortschakoff, the Russian Chancellor, to receive the deputation. They appealed for religious liberty not only in the States named but throughout Russia, making it plain that such liberty implied the sacred right of everyone to cherish, to profess and to propagate his religious convictions. They paid tribute to the Tsar for his action in liberating the serfs of Russia and pleaded for a like clemency in the religious sphere.

The Prince, in reply, claimed that religious liberty existed in Russia, except that members of the Orthodox Church were *not permitted to leave it*. This was a law which only the Emperor could change.

The interview bore some good fruit. The law was not altered, but its application was less rigorously enforced and some thousands of former converts returned to the Protestant Church.

It is pleasant to record that, in 1874, when the Tsar was visiting London, the Alliance transmitted to him an address expressing thanks for his having intervened in response to its appeal.

JAPAN

The year 1872 witnessed an interposition of the Alliance of an extraordinary character, being chiefly on behalf of Roman Catholics. Missionaries in Japan had sent a message to the Alliance, complaining of religious persecution and appealing for help. A deputation, therefore, headed by Lord Ebury, the President of the Alliance, was sent to interview Lord Granville, at that time the British Foreign Secretary. They complained, on the authority of the missionaries, that tablets bearing such inscriptions as "The Christian sect is strictly prohibited" had appeared on the principal buildings in all the cities of Japan, and that 4,000 native converts had been carried into exile, where they were suffering hardship. The custom of trampling on the cross was practised in the spring in many places.

Sir Harry Parkes, British Ambassador to Japan, read the translation of a document sent him by the Japanese Government, stating their desire to accord religious liberty to all subjects of Japan, unless their action constituted a threat to the Government or the authority of the Emperor.

Next year, when the Japanese Ambassadors arrived in Europe, they were met by representatives of the Paris Committee of the Alliance, who presented copies of the Scriptures to the Ambassadors. One of the members of the deputation gave the Ambassador to France a copy of the newly-published Gospel of St. John in Japanese. The Ambassador appeared to be highly pleased with it, and afterwards ordered forty copies of the Gospel to be purchased and distributed among the officials of the Embassy.

EGYPT

In 1876 Protestants in Egypt were undergoing severe persecution, their work obstructed and themselves cruelly treated by the Coptic sheikhs. In one case two men who had been reading the Bible in the house of a friend, were arrested on their way home and so terribly bastinadoed with a hippopotamus hide that one of them died.

The Alliance appealed to the British Foreign Office, which took the matter up and a memorial was presented to the Khedive of Egypt. As a result, he gave orders for the redress of grievances.

AUSTRIA

In 1879 the General Conference at Basle considered infringements of religious liberty which were taking place in Austria, and appointed a deputation to lay the matter before the Emperor Francis Joseph I. The Emperor received them and promised enquiry. The causes of complaint were removed, and the British Executive sent His Majesty a letter expressing gratitude for his interposition.

RUSSIA AGAIN

As the years drifted on, cases of persecution continued to be reported from Russia, and especially from the Baltic Provinces. At length, in 1888, the Evangelical Alliance appealed to the reigning Tsar and placed a memorial in his hands when he was visiting Denmark. His Majesty seems to have handed this memorial to M. Pobedonostzeff, the Procurator of the Holy Synod of the Orthodox Church.

This official, who was an arch-opponent of the Lutherans and other Protestants, made a reply from which a few quotations will throw light upon his attitude. "You ask for all sects," said the Procurator, "an equal and full liberty. Russia is convinced that nowhere in Europe do heterodox faiths, and even those which are not Christian, enjoy so full a liberty as in the bosom of the Russian people. But Europe does not know this. And why? Only because among you religious

Part of Letter of Thanks sent by the Council of the Alliance to the Shah of Persia for granting religious liberty (see page 69)

Design on Silk Handkerchief prepared to commemorate the founding of the Alliance in London, 1846

To His Imperial Majesty the Sultan Abd-ul-Aziz Khan.

May it please your Majesty.

The undersigned Memorialists, members of different nationalities, and of various Christian Churches united in the Evangelical Alliance by the bonds of a common faith, approach your Majesty with the expression of their highest respect.

They gratefully acknowledge the valuable concessions made to the cause of civil and religious liberty, which have shown the enlightened sentiments of your Imperial Government. They refer especially with much satisfaction, to a declaration made on a former occasion to the representative of Great Britain, that henceforward neither shall "Christianity be insulted in my dominions, nor shall Christians be in any way persecuted for their Religion;" and to the subsequent Hatti-Scheriff, declaring that "no subject of His Majesty the Sultan shall be hindered in the exercise of the religion that he professes, nor shall be in any way molested on that account."

Your Memorialists have learned, however, with feelings of deep regret that in some recent instances your Majesty's benevolent intentions have been frustrated; and that, contrary to the engagement entered into with several European Governments, the adoption of the Christian faith by some of your Majesty's subjects has been visited with cruel persecution on the part of certain Provincial Magistrates, who have thus acted in opposition to your Majesty's righteous and benevolent declarations.

They allude to the cases already brought before your Majesty's Government.

Three Ansairyeh converts to Christianity, who had been living peaceable and blameless lives as teachers in a Christian Mission School, were in September last suddenly seized, put in chains, and, after being denied food and drink, marched to Jebili, and thence to Damascus, where they were thrown into Prison, and have been (we are credibly informed) repeatedly beaten, reviled, and otherwise shamefully treated. No crime or offence against the law was brought against them, but on their refusal to abjure the Christian faith, they were enrolled in the Turkish army, and refused the exercise of Christian worship.

Your Memorialists are informed that, in consequence of representations made on behalf of these converts, orders have been given for their removal to Constantinople; but such removal whilst affording, possibly, some amelioration to their sad condition, would nevertheless involve banishment from their homes and families, and from the honorable employments in which they were engaged.

Another case is that of a father and son, who, because they avowed themselves Christians, were taken by the police from their homes at Marash, bound and brought under a strong guard to Aleppo, from whence they were subsequently removed to Constantinople, and put in prison. They have since, with the wife of the elder one, been banished to Smyrna; their three children, contrary to the wish of the parents, having been placed in a Moslem family, whose religious opinions are utterly opposed to their own convictions.

Your Memorialists are well aware of the numerous difficulties which your Majesty has to encounter in giving effect to the pledges of religious liberty so generously accorded a few years since. But they feel constrained to submit to your Majesty's notice, that the persecution of individuals for exercising their personal right to believe and worship according to their own free conscience, is both a violation of Treaty engagements, and at variance with the enlightened sentiments of civilized Nations.

Assured of your Majesty's gracious disposition, your Memorialists humbly, but earnestly, entreat that prompt and effective measures may be taken to redress the wrongs inflicted on your Majesty's Christian and loyal subjects, as above mentioned; that they may be recalled from banishment and restored to their homes and useful occupations; and that the officers of your Majesty's Government, in the provinces and elsewhere, may be charged to preserve free from molestation, and secure in the enjoyment of their religious privileges, any individuals whomsoever, professing Christianity, over whom, by your Majesty's appointment, they exercise authority.

Religious Liberty in Turkey
Letter to Appeal from the Alliance to the Sultan
(see pages 64-65)

liberty comprises also an absolute right to unlimited propagandism, and so you exclaim against our laws against those who pervert the faithful from orthodoxy. . . . In Russia the Western faiths are always ready to attack the power and unity of the country. Never will she allow the Orthodox Church to be robbed of her children."

And so Pobedonostzeff went on for years in the defence of the Established Church of his land, restricting the liberties of faiths not his own and subjecting to prison and exile men who could not but speak when conscience bade them do so.

ARMENIA

In 1893 the Mohammedans of Armenia rose against their Christian neighbours. An attempt was made to burn the American College at Marsovan and to place the blame on the Christians. Two of the native professors of the College were accused of sedition and of causing riots. These two Christian men – Thoumaian and Kayayan – were arrested and thrown into prison, among many others.

Madame Thoumaian sent an appeal to the Evangelical Alliance for help, and the Alliance turned to Lord Rosebery, the British Foreign Secretary, who made representations to the Turkish Government in the interests of a fair trial for the accused. The trial took place in Angora and resulted in the condemnation to death of Thoumaian, Kayayan and fifteen others, while yet others were sentenced to long imprisonments. Efforts were still made by the Alliance and the British Government on behalf of the two professors whose innocence appeared to be clear, and the Sultan commuted their sentences to exile. In sending them from Turkey he gave each of them a free pass to Brindisi and a present of £15. They came on to England, where they were received with rejoicing.

The troubles of Armenia, however, were not over and soon the world was shocked by the Armenian massacres. The Council of the Alliance expressed its deep concern and its sympathy with the oppressed, though it realised that the function of the Alliance was to deal with cases only in which the persecution was distinctly a religious one. Indeed, the Alliance was at that moment making strong representations to the Turkish Government, and to our own, respecting cases of such a nature, and a little later a special call to prayer for the Armenian Christians was issued.

SAXONY

Persecution of Methodists and Baptists having taken place, a deputation was sent by the Alliance to Dresden, where they had an interview with the Cultus Minister. The minister promised that steps should be taken without delay, to secure to the oppressed congregations State recognition and "a degree of religious liberty".

PORTUGAL

The twentieth century had only just begun when an outbreak of persecution of Protestants broke out in Portugal. While the various Protestant congregations in Lisbon were assembled for the Week of Prayer their representatives were summoned to the criminal court in the city and were told they must cease holding religious meetings on pain of prosecution. Later, the meeting of the Y.M.C.A. was stopped by the police.

Happily, the King of Portugal was that spring visiting Queen Victoria at Buckingham Palace, and the Evangelical Alliance arranged for a deputation, led by Lord Kinnaird, to wait upon him. The King received the deputation graciously and assured them that it was his wish that religious liberty should be granted to all Protestant Christians throughout his realm, and that he was determined to enforce this rule. This successful interview greatly helped the course of religious liberty on the Continent, and its influence was seen in the summer in Oporto in a very pleasant way. For the first time formal and public recognition was accorded to the Protestant schools at a patriotic demonstration. A Children's Festival, attended by a vast concourse of people, was held in the grounds of the Crystal Palace in that city. The Protestant children, with banners flying, were accommodated in the grandstand and sang several pieces. The ultra-clericals retired with their scholars when the turn of the Protestant children came, but the crowd remained and signified their appreciation by hearty applause.

A new thing had happened in Roman Catholic Portugal.

PERU

In 1912 the world was horrified by the revelation of atrocities committed by the rubber-gatherers of Putumayo and Peru upon the Indian natives.

Peru is nominally a Christian State and has in its constitution a clause according to which the State "protects the Roman Catholic Apostolic religion, and does not permit the public exercise of any other whatsoever".

The Evangelical Alliance protested strongly and repeatedly against the atrocities and against the intolerant regime under which they were committed, and it is reassuring to note that in time the atrocities ceased and Protestant mission work has been fostered.

SPAIN

In the same year, 1912, a gross violation of religious liberty occurred in Spain. A young army officer, Pablo Fernandez, of Evangelical faith, begged his superior not to send him to Mass, but the superior officer insisted on his going. Faced with the dilemma of either kneeling with his companions in arms at the elevation of the Host or of obeying his conscience, Fernandez preferred to suffer rather than to do what he felt to be wrong. For not kneeling he was court-martialled. The Evangelical Alliance appealed on his behalf to the Spanish Prime Minister, who replied sympathetically.

The court-martial acquitted Fernandez, but the Captain-General refused to confirm the acquittal and the case had to go before the Supreme Military Tribunal in Madrid. The higher court condemned Fernandez to six months' imprisonment. The Evangelical Alliance made appeal to the new Premier who had come into office, urging him to advise the King to exercise the royal clemency towards the prisoner. Soon afterwards the news came to hand that the King of Spain had, on the Premier's recommendation, granted a free pardon to Fernandez, promising in addition that steps should be taken to free Spanish soldiers and sailors from the obligation of attending Mass.

In the same year another instance in Spain of the violation

of religious liberty attracted attention throughout Protestant Europe.

Juan Labrador, a Colonel in the Spanish Marines, was appointed to preside at a court-martial. Now this involved attending at the Mass of the Holy Spirit, with its adoration of the Wafer. Colonel Labrador, as a Presbyterian and a member of the Evangelical Alliance, felt he could not conscientiously do this. He appealed to be exempted, but was refused. He therefore declined to attend and was prosecuted. The prosecuting counsel demanded a sentence of six years' imprisonment, but the court-martial, regretting that it could not legally acquit him, imposed six months only and petitioned the King for a pardon. The Spanish branch of the Alliance also petitioned King Alfonso for a free pardon, and this His Majesty granted.

A Bill was at once introduced into the Spanish Parliament, doing away in the Navy with compulsory attendance at the Mass of the Holy Spirit.

MALTA

In 1925 the Council of the Alliance was troubled by Roman Catholic opposition to its mission in Malta and followed carefully the discussion of the new constitution of the island. This constitution laid down that all persons in Malta should have full liberty of conscience and free exercise of worship. The Malta Parliament, however, under priestly influence, petitioned the King that it should be stated that "the religion of Malta is the Roman Catholic Apostolic religion" and that persons might be excluded by reason of their religious profession from the Departments of Public Instruction and Education. The Colonial Secretary, happily, did not see his way to advise the King to accede to these requests.

SPAIN, 1929

Years passed over Spain, but the intolerant spirit of Rome persisted, and in 1929 the victim was a woman, Carmen Padin, who had declared her belief that the Virgin Mary had other children beside our Lord, a belief for which she could naturally refer to the New Testament. However, she was arrested and tried. The Spanish Committee of the Alliance brought the matter to the attention of the London Executive, who sent out money to meet the expenses of the trial. The issue was a sentence of two years' imprisonment.

During the imprisonment the Spanish branch of the Alliance arranged for a regular supply to be given her, and at length Carmen Padin was released from prison. The release, however, was accompanied by a sentence of banishment from her village. So petty and so persistent was the pursuit of this humble, Christian woman.

BRAZIL

In 1931 the Alliance organ published a significant incident related in *South America* by Mr. F. C. Glass, of North Brazil. A Protestant colporteur visited a Brazilian town which is the seat of a Roman Catholic bishopric. Spreading his Bibles, Testaments and Gospels on a ground cloth, he began to speak of the importance of reading the Bible, and was offering a Gospel for a cent, when three priests interrupted him and ordered him to leave the place. The colporteur replied that he was a free Brazilian citizen and was protected by the free constitution of his country.

At this, one of the priests mounted a stall and fiercely denounced him. "There is no time to lose," shouted the priest. "Beat him!" The mob fell on the colporteur, tore his coat from him, attacked him with sticks and stones, and destroyed his Scriptures and bag. He had almost succumbed when a soldier drew his weapon and defended him.

The colporteur's life was thus saved, but the criminal priest remained at liberty and no restitution was made. Such is the attitude of Rome, in many a missionary sphere, towards those who seek to spread the Word of God.

THE YEAR 1937

In spite of the growing lip-homage paid to the principle of religious liberty, the Alliance had in 1937 to draw attention to outbursts of persecution in three different parts of the world – Japan, Rumania and Italy. These represented the action of rulers professing widely-differing religious creeds – Shinto, Orthodox, Romanist – all of whom found their policies thwarted by the conscience of Christians seeking to walk in the way marked out by their Saviour.

THE WAR YEARS, 1939–1945

In the Second World War, fought by the Allies to secure liberty of life, the chief freedom from the Evangelical standpoint was freedom of religion – freedom to believe, to worship and to propagate one's faith according to conscience.

Great interest was aroused in 1943 by the news of Marshal Stalin's recognition, and restoration, of the Russian Orthodox Church. The Evangelical Alliance welcomed the news in the hope that the consideration shown to the Orthodox Church was intended to apply to all Christian Churches in the Soviet realm. The present situation, however, is not yet clarified.

In the meantime, anxiety was caused by events in Spain, where many churches were closed and it was forbidden to print, import, or circulate the Bible. Some pastors and Evangelists were put in prison. Protestant day schools were being closed and children of Protestant parents sent to State schools, where they were compelled to venerate the image of the Virgin Mary and to learn the Roman Catholic catechism.

The Evangelical Alliance Executive took active steps to bring the position before the authorities, and, it is to be hoped, not without success. The latest reports are brighter.

THE END OF THE WAR

With the end of the war intense relief was felt by Evangelical believers that the power of the Nazi, Fascist and Japanese tyrannies had been broken, and a new opportunity given for the establishment of religious freedom in lands which had been denied it.

As the time for the San Francisco Conference drew near, the Executive of the Evangelical Alliance sent an earnest appeal to the British Foreign Office that freedom of conscience and worship should be included in the programme of the nations. This appeal was favourably received.

Then, when the new Parliament for Great Britain had been elected, a letter emphasising the importance of religious freedom was addressed by the Alliance to all the members in each House.

Thus, throughout the first century of its life, the Alliance has been true to its historical purpose as a champion of religious liberty.

Our review will also have shown how precious that liberty is which has cost so much in human suffering; how constant is the danger to liberty from tyrannous authorities; and how necessary that those who possess spiritual freedom should give sympathy and active help to those who have it not.

CHAPTER IX

THE ALLIANCE AND THE LORD'S DAY

AT the Liverpool Conference held in 1845 to prepare for the founding of the Alliance the question of the Lord's Day was debated. Some thought the Day of Rest should be included as a divine ordinance in the basis of the Alliance: others considered its observance should be placed among the "objects" of the Alliance, for the realisation of which earnest effort should be made. This latter view prevailed and was approved by the Inaugural Conference in 1846.

The importance of this subject was specially impressed on the mind of John Henderson, the Scottish merchant who, more than any other, may be considered the founder of the Alliance. He at once devised a scheme for a series of tracts on the Sabbath by ministers of different denominations. His plan was adopted, and tracts were written by Ralph Wardlaw, James Hamilton, Edward Bickersteth, John Angell James and others. The tracts were published in a volume entitled *The Christian Sabbath*. A copy of this book, with an inscription in the handwriting of John Henderson, describing the Sabbath as "the shrine and the safeguard of all our religious advantages", is preserved in the library of the Alliance.

So successful did this series of tracts prove that Mr. Henderson was encouraged to go farther, and the idea occurred to him of engaging the working classes in the discussion and defence of the Sabbath. He therefore offered three prizes, of £25, £15 and £10, respectively, for the best essays to be written by working men on the temporal advantages to themselves of the Sabbath. Three months only were allowed for their preparation, but so great was the interest evoked that in that time no fewer than 1,045 essays were produced, as a recorder tells, "from hands that were employed all day in casting the shuttle or delving the mine, in holding the plough or wielding the mallet and the chisel".

Many of these essays revealed high ability and true piety. It was felt by the promoters that they had opened in the heart of labouring Britain "a vein of rich and precious ore".

THE ALLIANCE AND THE LORD'S DAY 81

One of the most remarkable essays was the work of a Scottish labourer's daughter, and was felt to be so valuable that the authoress was asked to consent to its separate publication and to prepare a sketch of her life to be prefixed to it To this she consented and the book *The Pearl of Days* was the result.

The interest in the movement was now so keen that it was felt that more prizes must be awarded, and a hundred more, of £5 each, were offered. Among the donors were the Prince Consort, who contributed ten prizes, the Archbishop of Canterbury, Lord Ashley (later Lord Shaftesbury); and Sir Culling Eardley, the Alliance President.

The effort was by this time a national one, and the Queen was approached to secure her approval. This she willingly accorded, and gave permission for *The Pearl of Days* to be dedicated to Her Majesty. The essay-writers included workers in many trades – joiners, carpenters and cabinet-makers (51), printers (48), shoemakers (41), weavers (39), tailors (33), agricultural labourers (21), gardeners (24), blacksmiths (17), miners (12), etc.

Within a few months 30,000 copies of *The Pearl of Days* were sold, and it has since been translated into several foreign languages. At the close of 1848 a public meeting to distribute the prizes was held in Exeter Hall, presided over by Lord Ashley, who was commissioned by the Prince Consort to present his prizes for him. Several of the prize-winners addressed the meeting, and as time went on many of the essay, were published, under such titles as *The Light of the Weeks The Torch of Time, The Stream in the Desert, The Pilgrim's Arbour on the Way to Glory*.

The movement had given a valuable stimulus to the observance of the sacred day.

In the same year this great question engaged the attention of a session of the annual Conference of the German Evangelical Alliance, held at Stuttgart. An address upon it by Prof. Schmid, of Tubingen University, was followed by discussion and the passing of a resolution, (I) To publish an address to the German people on the duty and benefit of Sabbath "sanctification", and (2) To petition the several Governments of Germany in favour of legal regulations for a fitting observance of the day.

In 1856 a deputation, initiated by the Alliance and headed by the Archbishop of Canterbury, waited on Lord Palmerston, then Prime Minister, to appeal against proposals for opening the British Museum and the Crystal Palace on Sunday. Two of the most impressive addresses were delivered by a plumber and a coal-porter. Lord Palmerston promised the consideration of his Cabinet.

Five years later, at the Geneva Conference of the Alliance, the observance of the Lord's Day was the special topic and action was taken which led to the formation of committees for its promotion in several of the Swiss cities. Many manufacturers of watches and jewellery and tradesmen of various kinds consented to close their establishments on Sunday, and the Swiss Government agreed to discontinue public works on that day.

So great and so abiding was the impression created at this Conference that fifteen years afterwards, in 1876, it was resolved to hold in Geneva a still more representative Conference to consider the question in its international aspects. In this assembly delegates from many nations and varied interests took part; the German Emperor sent his ambassador, General Roder; the Paris and Lyons Railway its Inspector-General; the Rumanian Railways their Chairman; the Genevan Consuls of American and European States were present, besides editors of newspapers, lawyers, bankers and other men of influence in the business world. The Conference occupied three days and plans were passed for the creation of an International Confederation for the revival of the observance of the Lord's Day.

Next day, Sunday, the churches of Geneva were crowded to hear sermons on the subject, and in the evening 3,000 persons assembled in the Hall of the Reformation to listen to addresses upon it by M. Edouard Monod and M. E. Naville. Deeply impressive was the singing of verses composed by M. Monod:

Jour du repos! Jour du Seigneur!
(Day of rest! Day of the Lord!)

This remarkable Conference was followed two years later by another, called to consider the same theme. During the Paris Exhibition of 1878 a large concourse met in the Salle Evangelique and listened to informing and inspirational addresses on the Lord's Day.

THE ALLIANCE AND THE LORD'S DAY

In 1880 an interesting account of Sunday in the White House was quoted in the Alliance organ from a Washington journalist. At that time Mr. Hayes was President of the United States and in his home Sunday was felt to be one of the pleasantest days of the week. "The family", writes this witness, "invariably attend church in the morning, and as many of the inmates as desire. The meals are so arranged that the servants can attend if they choose." The writer goes on to describe the evening of the day when the Vice-President and his Secretary and a few other friends arrive and join Mr. and Mrs. Hayes and the family in hymns and sacred music. Happy the nation in which, from White House or from Palace, such an example is given!

As years passed, it became clear that the true observance of the Day of Rest could only be preserved as the result of vigilance and action. Repeated attempts were made to introduce organised games and amusements on Sunday. These were strenuously resisted by the Evangelical Alliance, and when, in 1922, the London County Council was being urged to open at least two of the public parks of London for recreation the Alliance called a great meeting in Queen's Hall, to consider "Sunday Observance: A National Obligation and Responsibility". In the meantime the L.C.C. had refused to sanction the Sunday games, and their attitude was warmly approved by the meeting, in which Lord Haddo, the Chairman, described the Fourth Commandment as "a charter of freedom for the weakest and humblest in the earth", for it called for rest on the Holy Day for the manservant and the maidservant.

Later, however, the London County Council reversed its policy and opened the parks for Sunday games. To this a telling rejoinder was made in a letter to the Press by the Rev. R. C. Gillie, Hon. Secretary of the Evangelical Alliance. It was then resolved to give the public an opportunity of expressing its mind, and a new meeting was called at Queen's Hall early in 1923. So overwhelming was the attendance at this that great numbers failed to gain admission and an overflow meeting was held in All Souls' Church, Langham Place. At both meetings a resolution was unanimously passed protesting against Sunday games in the parks and urging all citizens to unite in the defence of Sunday as the Day of Rest and Worship.

The Alliance Council followed up these protests with a

vigorous campaign to make them effective, and it was a significant fact that many of the chief cities of Britain refused in this matter to follow the lead given by the capital.

In 1924 the British Empire Exhibition was held in the vicinity of London and the Alliance Executive expressed its thankfulness that the directors decided that the Exhibition should not be open on Sundays, thus setting free the multitude of employees for rest and, if they so wished, for worship. Next year the same wise rule obtained for the continued Exhibition.

Within the last few years the Alliance has taken an active part in opposing the Sunday opening of theatres, and in this support has been given by a large number of actors and actresses who have protested against the loss of their rest-day.

The battle continues, for the enemies of the Lord's Day never sleep. The Alliance sees in the neglect of its observance a root-cause of the troubles of our time. Without the hallowing of this day there come the loss of spiritual vision, the blunting of conscience and the disuse of worship, with the lessening of the sense of God. No better celebration of the Alliance centenary could be found than the world-wide revival of the keeping of the Holy Day.

CHAPTER X

DEFENCE OF THE FAITH

OPPOSITION TO MOVEMENTS CHALLENGING THE GOSPEL

1. INFIDELITY

AT the formation of the Alliance it was agreed that one of its prime objects should be the defence of the faith against movements challenging it, and that among these Infidelity should have a prominent place. In the debate on the subject, J. G. Oncken, of Hamburg, told of the growing boldness of Infidelity in Germany, and mentioned that in Hamburg a newspaper announcement had been made of a Sunday performance in which a person named would relate a conversation he had held with the devil in hell. (This statement produced a sensation in the meeting.)

In accordance with the decision of the Conference, the Alliance has throughout its career dealt with this question and in 1849 offered prizes of £20 and £15 for the best essays on the principles and operations of Infidelity among the working classes. The competitors were themselves to be members of these classes; the desire being to ascertain what infidel opinions were rife among working people, the causes and effects of such opinions, and the best remedy to be employed.

In order to reach the wider public, a further offer was made of £100 for the best essay on the general operations of Infidelity, whether British or foreign.

Excellent essays in each division were sent in.

But the Alliance was not content simply to elicit the opinions of others on the subject, and in 1855 at the Paris Conference a session was devoted to it and a notable address upon it was delivered by M. de Pressense. Starting with Deism in England in the eighteenth century, he suggested that England, wearied with the political quarrels of the seventeenth century, imagined God to be far off, not caring about the petty affairs of men. Voltaire, he continued, brought Deism to France and with his brilliant gifts made it popular; Rousseau added to it a touch of sentimentality and it was among the causes of the French Revolution. Then the speaker turned to German Rationalism, which, starting with Kant, moved step by step, through Fichte, Schelling and Hegel, to Pantheistic Humanism, which left no room for divine personality or the human will. God was the world; the world was God; above all man was God. In this we of a later age see the link between eighteenth century unbelief and the scientific Humanism of to-day.

In his closing paragraph M. de Pressense asked why Infidelity had made such progress, and prominent among its causes he found the reaction against Roman Catholic formality, hardness and cruelty. Rome, he felt, was a "living calumny" of the Gospel and through it Christianity had been falsely judged. Yet some blame, he realised, was due to other Churches, which had not shown "a complete Christianity" and had been too much absorbed in their disputes. It was time to "man the ramparts" in the defence, not only of the supernatural, but of conscience, moral liberty, and every element of the religious life.

For practical work against Infidelity a Swiss Evangelical Union was formed in 1872, and at a meeting of this Union the chair was taken by an eminent physician who himself had been a Rationalist, but had been converted to Christian belief largely through witnessing the death-bed of Dr. Cesar Malan. He there saw a strength against suffering and a peace in prospect of death such as, he felt, his own "religion" could not supply. He sought, and found, it in the Lord Jesus Christ.

In 1873 the Alliance at its assembly in Brighton gave a session to this subject and one speaker told of the discussions at the Hall of Science, in which many advocates of Atheism had been defeated. After the lapse of seven decades we may ask, "Where is the Hall of Science now?"

In 1877 the Alliance organ reported a conference on the subject held at Lambeth Palace, in which Prebendary Row recommended that the Universities should insist on a fuller study of Christian Evidences, and the Archbishop of Canterbury advocated the circulation of the great healthy literature of England as one of the best antidotes to Infidelity.

In 1880, at an Alliance Conference in Nottingham, Dr. Sinclair Paterson spoke on "Christian Philosophies and False Philosophies", showing how effectively Christian belief, resting on Holy Scripture, could hold its own against resting on Infidelity.

So with the years the stream of testimony went on until 1941, when the Alliance, through its magazine, pointed out how the Nietzsche philosophy had borne evil fruit in German life and thought, and at length in the Second World War which was even then devastating the world. To Nietzsche, as later to Hitler, the Christian teaching of humility and love was a "slave morality"; might was right, a doctrine upon which a terrible light has been thrown in our day.

Well did the prize-winning working man of 1850 take for the motto of his essay on Infidelity the words "Shadow of Death".

2. SPIRITUALISM

The Alliance has repeatedly taken the field against Spiritualism, a movement found in all ages of human history, which has had an extraordinary revival in modern times. The bereavements caused by two great wars have caused intense interest in the question of the after-life, and a deep desire in many hearts for intercourse, if that is possible, with dear ones in the unseen. The result has been the multiplication of "Spirit seances" and the issue of numerous spiritualist books and papers. Many who turn to Spiritualism are sincere and honourable, but they depend on evidence which is unreliable and has, in many cases, been found to be fraudulent.

The Alliance has opposed Spiritualism by publishing pamphlets against it, such as Bishop Hasse's *Spiritualism, Its Character, Teaching and Effects*, and Sir Robert Anderson's *Spirit Manifestations*. Bishop Hasse points out that intercourse with spirits is forbidden in Scripture (e.g. in Leviticus xix. 31 and xx. 27), and that if spirits do indeed speak through the mediums at seances, they cannot be good spirits obedient to the will of God. He points out also that the "revelations" they are supposed to make are invariably trivial, bringing us no real knowledge of the life of the hereafter. He refers with deep respect to Sir Oliver Lodge, whose loss of his son Raymond led him into spiritualistic practices of which he has published an account. The communications, however, purporting to have come from Raymond are shown to have been worthless; Raymond telling of "silly spirits who wanted a game"; of "sky-larking"; of a "nice doggie that twists about"; of cigars and whisky and soda which some newly-arrived spirits "would have" and which were manufactured out of "essences and ethers and gases".

Then Hasse touches on the danger of Spiritualism – on the beclouding of intellect and conscience so often caused by it, and quotes the declaration of Dr. Forbes Winslow that "Ten thousand unfortunate people are at the present time confined in lunatic asylums on account of having tampered with the supernatural".

The Alliance also issued an article dealing appreciatively with Miss Jane T. Stoddart's book, *The Case Against Spiritualism*, and quoting from it her judgment: "We believe that mental and moral harm may result from 'borderland' studies, because in these the personality is peculiarly liable to the loss of will-power and self-control. We shall do well to keep the doors of the soul shut until we can open them to God."

The Alliance does not ask the testimony of Spiritualism as to the future life. It rests on the word of Christ, who declared Himself to be the Resurrection and the Life, who promised to His disciples a place in the mansions of His Father's House, and who by His own victory over the grave became "the first-fruits of them that are asleep".

3. THEOSOPHY

The strange system of Theosophy, put forth by Madame Blavatsky, was also opposed in the Alliance organ. Its wide but transient popularity in the eighteen-nineties was largely due to its clever advocacy by Mrs. Annie Besant. It was really an old-world philosophy, mainly Buddhist, brought out by Madame Blavatsky in the United States as the basis of a Society. It regarded the universe as having come into existence through an impersonal principle, in which there was no room for the God of Christianity. It taught the reincarnation of man age after age, the incarnations linked by "Karma", the sequence of cause and effect, through which a man's position and character in any given life are fixed by his deeds in an earlier life. It rested its teaching on the supposed testimony of "Mahatmas" ("great spirits") who had passed through many incarnations and who had appeared in evening hours on the margin of Indian waters to believers in Theosophy. Wonderful things, such as the ringing of bells and the precipitation of roses without material cause, were said to be done by Theosophists through their control of occult forces. The Evangelical Alliance meets Theosophy with the revealed Word of the living God, made known supremely through the perfect life of His incarnate Son, a life not spent in shadowy retreats, but in the midst of men in village and in city. It declares the power of faith in the once-crucified Redeemer to blot out the guilt and habit of sin, and it finds its evidences not in "occult phenomena", but in the renewed lives of men and women who were servants of sin but have been regenerated and sanctified by the Spirit of God.

4. CHRISTIAN SCIENCE

Another religious philosophy resisted by the Evangelical Alliance is the well-known "Christian Science". In this system of thought, presented in Mrs. Eddy's book *Science and Health* (published in 1875), there is a mingling of truth with error. In an article by the Rev. E. L. Langston, in the Alliance organ, it is pointed out that Christian Science emphasises the power of mind, the possibility of divine healing and the development of the spiritual life. But Mr. Langston shows that the effect of these truths is spoiled by the false doctrines that matter does not exist and that sin and disease are only figments of the mind. Christian Science denies the real humanity of our Lord Jesus, and rejects His deity, atonement and resurrection.

Mr. Langston sums up his judgment of it in the words: "It is a religion without a Personal God, without Salvation, without Sacraments, and speaks lightly concerning sin, marriage and judgment to come."

Second only to the moral and religious defects of Christian Science is the physical aspect of a theory which denies the reality of disease and tends to cause refusal of medical aid to the sick and dying. Upon the whole subject Mr. Langston quotes the grave words of Pandita Ramabai, the well-known Indian convert to Christianity, who when she learned the teaching of Christian Science said: "I recognised it as being the same philosophy that has been taught my people for

4,000 years. It has wrecked millions of lives and caused immeasurable suffering and sorrow in my land."

5. THE NEW THEOLOGY

Forty years ago the Churches of Britain received a shock through the preaching of what was called "The New Theology" by the occupant of one of the most famous of London pulpits. The teaching was not really new, for it had been repeatedly put forth, and rejected, in earlier ages, but it was new to the many who were familiar only with Evangelical doctrine.

The principles of "The New Theology" were published in 1907 in a book bearing that title. They implied the abandonment of accepted Christian beliefs as to the authority of the Bible, the unique divinity of Christ, the essential evil of sin, and the value of the atoning work of Christ in putting sin away.

The Alliance Executive was deeply concerned at this teaching and arranged for the publication of a number of pamphlets answering it. Among the writers of these were Prebendary Webb-Peploe, on *Sin and its Consequences*; Rev. W. Fuller Gooch, on *Salvation – What It Is*; Dr. James Orr, on *The Virgin Birth*; Rev. Harrington C. Lees, on *Man in Relation to God*; Canon Girdlestone, on *The Resurrection of Christ*; and Dr. G. Hanson, on *The Impregnable Rock – Christ Jesus*.

It is pleasant to be able to record that after some time the author of *The New Theology* recalled his book and reverted to a more evangelical message, in the proclamation of which he is now held in honour.

6. BAHAISM

In 1934 the Alliance drew attention to a Moslem sect which was claiming to put forth a new world-religion. In an article in the Alliance organ by the Rev. J. R. Richards, of Persia, an account of the movement was given. It was founded, it appears, by a Persian exile in Baghdad, who took to himself the title "Bahaullah" (Splendour of God). Bahaullah drew up a new code of laws to which he gave the name of "The

Most Holy Book", and he appealed to the Christian Scriptures for proofs of the truth of his new faith.

"Bahaism", as it was now called, spread to Europe, being introduced to France by a Jew who gave it a rationalistic turn; it found some converts in England, and crossed the Atlantic to America, where it took on an allegorical form in which Bahaullah appeared as the Incarnation of God; Abdul Baha, the leader then living, being regarded as Christ returned.

The article makes clear that Bahaism is a denial of all that is fundamental in Christianity. Its teaching about God is pantheistic: the human soul is "a transitory appearance of the divine"; evil has no real existence. Christ's virgin birth, atoning death, resurrection and ascension are all denied. He was "only a prophet who came to pave the way for the coming of Bahaullah". Abdul Baha dreamed of a Bahai world, but after a brief success the movement has already to a large extent declined. Many of its assemblies have ended and its Sunday Schools have closed down.

7. THE STAR IN THE EAST

Another Asiatic movement to which attention has been drawn by the Alliance is "The Order of the Star in the East", which arose in India under the influence of Mrs. Besant, who had passed from Theosophy to Hinduism.

An account of this movement given in the Alliance magazine shows that its idea is to prepare for the coming of an expected World Teacher. Founded in Benares in 1911, it had in two years 12,000 enrolled members, said to be drawn from all the world's great religions. It has no definite belief as to who the Coming One will be. Some have been looking for Christ, and some for Krishna.

The Alliance looks for One only, who has said that He will come again, the Saviour and the Judge, who is to be King of kings.

8. MILLENNIAL DAWINISM

This movement arose in 1872, being founded in the United States by Charles T. Russell, who became widely known as "Pastor Russell" An able organiser, with a great faith in advertisement, he gained numerous adherents. The Alliance magazine, *Evangelical Christendom*, drew attention to the movement through a criticism penned by an American writer, Dr. Haldemann, who condemned its teaching as erroneous in regard to the Person of Christ, who was said to have ceased to be a man at the moment when He died on the Cross. According to this theory, therefore, our Lord did not carry our human nature up into heaven and will not come again as a man.

The teaching as to the Atonement also was condemned as misleading. Russell died in 1916, but the movement has continued and is now known as "Jehovah's Witnesses". It is incorporated in New York and Pennsylvania as "The Watchtower Bible and Tract Society."

CHAPTER XI

THE ALLIANCE AND ITS CARE FOR DEPRESSED RACES

THE Evangelical Alliance has realised from the first that its supreme business is with the spiritual aspects of life – drawing Christians into unity; preaching the Gospel; winning men and women to God. But it has also realised that this great function implies care for the whole man, the securing for him of daily conditions in which the life of the soul can prosper. It has a battle with injustice and cruelty everywhere.

SLAVERY

We have seen how at the Foundation Conference of the Alliance strong feeling was expressed against slavery, but that owing to the delicate position on the subject then existing among the American Churches it was decided not to make "Anti-Slavery" an item in the basis of the Alliance. So the question was left to the action of the Christian conscience.

There was, however, no doubt as to the attitude of the men of the Conference to slavery and to the negro race, as was shown in the warm reception given to the negro pastor.

In 1861 the Civil War between the North and the South, in which slavery was the crucial question, broke out and people in the United States and even in England were drawn up on the two sides.

The position of the Alliance was at once made clear in an article which appeared in *Evangelical Christendom* in 1861. It was the review of a book on *Slavery and the Southern States of America*, but it rose to the fullness and authority of a great manifesto. It begins by quoting a letter from Virginia: "The South possess nearly four millions of slaves, worth on an average £150 each. That is to say," goes on the writer, "there are nearly four millions of the inhabitants of the South who are destitute, by the circumstances of their birth, of every personal, social and civil right. These four millions of human beings have their value in the market, precisely like oxen, sheep, or swine: they are defined as "property", worth in the gross some £600,000,000."

The writer shows how the work in the cotton-fields by these unpaid labourers has built up great fortunes, and produced an idle and debased class of owners while plunging the negro serfs into a moral and social abyss. Some of the social results of the system are hinted at.

The article draws to a close by referring to the astonishing fact that many Christian men, and even leaders, were tainted with this evil, like a Bishop, who was said to possess four hundred slaves. So in a restrained but urgent manner the writer presents a great call to the Christian conscience for justice to the oppressed and the freeing of a captive multitude to the hearing and obeying of the Gospel.

The story of the emancipated slaves, with its upgrowth of negro churches and great coloured conventions reveals the rebound of a race toward God when once the restraining forces have been taken away. The negro brings his own contribution to the Kingdom of God. He has the gifts of song and speech; he possesses a wealth of imagination, emotion and affection. His "negro spirituals" go directly to the human heart. With childlike frankness he is open to the appeal of the cross, and the Church needs him to make up the fullness of her fellowship. The Evangelical Alliance is set for the claiming of every race for Christ and for the overthrow of all that hinders "the brother for whom Christ died".

But the defeat of slavery in the Southern States of America did not end slavery in the world. Africa, from which the American slaves had been kidnapped, was for many years the scene of cruel slave raids conducted by Arabs, and again and again the Evangelical Alliance stepped forward as the champion of the oppressed. This was shown with historical detail at the Jubilee of the Alliance in London by Mr. Heli Chatelain, a leader in the cause of the African. He began by referring to the visit paid by many of the delegates to the tomb of David Livingstone, in Westminster Abbey, and to the words carved on the slab that covers it – words among the last he wrote – "All I can add in my solitude is, May Heaven's rich blessing come down on everyone – American, English, or Turk – who will help to heal this open sore of the world."

These words, written of the African slave trade, were declared by the speaker to be no exaggeration of the evil. He told of the coming of the Arab slavers into a peaceful African village, of their winning of the confidence of the trustful natives by gifts of trinkets, then of their seizing of their opportunity to loot the village, killing resisters and marching off the young men and women in chains to the slave-mart, on the way to which many would succumb and fall a prey to wild beasts. It was estimated that 500,000 lives were annually sacrificed to the slave trade.

The appeals of Livingstone roused the conscience of the civilised world, and by the Brussels Act, which took effect in 1873, the Colonial Powers assumed the duty not only of liberating the slaves but of caring for them afterwards.

This favourable attitude of the political powers opened a new door of opportunity to the Christian Church and the Evangelical Alliance became the first Protestant body to encourage the organisation of national leagues of liberation. The International Council of the Alliance in Berlin invited the branches of the Alliance to take up the cause, with the result of the formation in Germany of the African International League, which started what is said to have been the first settlement of liberated slaves in East Africa.

Then, in 1891, the General Conference of the Alliance at Florence supported the movement and a Swiss Society was formed, while in the United States a Liberators' League came into being, among the founders of which were six officers of the American Evangelical Alliance.

Yet while all this was going on a sharp battle with slavery was taking place in Central Africa, as is shown by an interesting note in the Alliance organ in 1887. "The new expedition", it remarks, "undertaken under the leadership of Mr. H. M. Stanley, is one in which we are bound to take a deep interest, both for the sake of humanity and of the Gospel. The deeply lamented General Gordon had it at heart to destroy the odious and cruel slave trade. . . . He sent an officer far away to the South, towards the sources of the Nile for the purpose of endeavouring to put some stop to this most abominable traffic. . . . That officer has succeeded in establishing order and government in his province, which lies immediately north of the great lake Albert Nyanza. The Arab slave traders, however, have surrounded and shut him in, and the object of the expedition is to carry to him relief and deliverance. Those Arabs have extended their power to the Congo, and have swept down on the settlement at Stanley Falls...."

"It is evident that much will have to be done and much endured before the Dark Continent is brought under the beneficial sway of the blessed Saviour, but the Church of Christ must not and will not abandon the enterprise till the banner of the Cross waves over those wide-spread regions which from time immemorial have been the gloomy habitations of cruelty."

DOMESTIC SLAVERY

Even when the slave trade was done away, domestic slavery continued to exist in many parts of Africa. This was the case in Uganda until the Gospel brought it to an end. A speaker at the Alliance Jubilee Congress in 1896 told how this came about. One of the domestic slaves, a small boy, had been ill-treated by his master and ran away, taking refuge with a Christian chief. According to the law of Uganda at that time the boy had to be given up to his cruel master. But the Christian chief hesitated and with a number of other chiefs sought the advice of their missionary, Bishop Tucker.

The Bishop refused to express an opinion, but read to them passages from the New Testament, bidding us to "love one another".

The chiefs went away, but came back in a few days with a letter signed by about forty of them, asking that their country might have the full privileges of freedom. The result was the ending of domestic slavery in Uganda.

CENTENARY OF THE ABOLITION OF SLAVERY IN THE BRITISH EMPIRE

In 1933 the Alliance joined in the celebration of the centenary of the abolition of slavery in the British Empire. An article in *Evangelical Christendom* recalled the terrors of the "Middle Passage" between Africa and the New World, in which the first ship to sail from Britain was the "Jesus". The "Middle Passage" became indeed the Calvary of the negro race. Britain's share in this infamous traffic was to transport

*Eleventh International Conference, London, 1907
Conference Group at Trent Park, New Barnet
(see page 107)*

80th Anniversary Celebrations, 1927
Back row, left to right: Rev. D. G. Hanson, Rev. W. F. Gooch, Rev. The Hon. W. Talbot Rice, Pastor Hoyois (Belgium), Rev. Dr. R. C. Gillie, Canon H. Foster Pegg, Rev. T. J. ulvertaft, Rev. J. Chalmers Lyon, Professor Hamaradka (Czechoslovakia), Mr. H. M. Gooch, Mr. Jacques Hopkins. Front row: Mr. A. H. Habershon, Rev. Adam Podin (Esthonia), Rev. Fernando Cabrera (Spain), Pastor Cavaliere Ugo Janni (Italy), Herr G. F. Nagel (Germany), Mr. R. C. Hart-Dyke, Mrs. Hart-Dyke, Dr. Stegegna (Holland), Mrs. Hamaradka. (see pages 110-111)

3,000,000 negroes in a century, of whom it was estimated that 250,000 were thrown into the Atlantic.

At last came the awakening of the public conscience through the appeals of Wilberforce and his comrades, and the trade was abolished. In 1833 any slave who took refuge under the Union Jack was declared to be free.

Not even yet, however, was slavery destroyed throughout the world, for it was estimated that there were still 5,000,000 slaves in various countries, and the Evangelical Alliance called on Christians everywhere to impress upon governments the urgent need of action for the setting of all these captives free.

Wilberforce had died in 1833, a month before the passing of the Emancipation Bill, and the Executive of the Alliance passed a resolution in which they did honour to the memory of the great liberator, while also paying tribute to the British Government of the day and to the Anti-Slavery Society for the efforts they were making to complete his work.

THE NATIVE RACES AND THE LIQUOR TRAFFIC

It is not only, however, in connection with slavery that the Evangelical Alliance has shown its care for the depressed races. It has strongly opposed the liquor traffic through which intoxicating drink has been imported into Africa with demoralising results to the natives. When this trade was in debate, *Evangelical Christendom* denounced it as "an obstacle to moral and religious progress".

CHAPTER XII

THE ALLIANCE AND MISSIONS

ALTHOUGH the Alliance was not founded as a missionary society, its spirit has always been intensely missionary, and it has worked in warm fellowship with the missionary societies of the various denominations. At the centre of its life has stood the Cross which commands the world, and it has cherished in its heart the loving devotion to Christ which inspires the carrying of His Gospel to every man.

The quality of a movement can be gauged by the kind of men it chooses to lead it, and it is significant that the new Evangelical Alliance, in 1846, chose as its first President Sir Culling Eardley, the Treasurer of the London Missionary Society. Sir Culling continued till his death in 1863 to be the human link between the two societies, bringing to the Evangelical Alliance the inspiration of an immediate contact with the victories of Christianity in heathen lands, and to the Missionary Society the sense of the breadth and strength of the Christian fellowship.

The warm feeling of the Alliance towards Missions was expressed at its foundation in a resolution proposed by the Rev. W. Arthur, author of *The Tongue of Fire*, and seconded by Dr. Cumming, of Crown Court. In this resolution the members of the Conference declared their longing for the universal spread of Christ's kingdom; gave praise to God for the grace whereby, in late years, Christians had been moved to missionary effort; offered their fraternal congratulations and sympathy to all Evangelical missionaries; and prayed that through the outpouring of the Holy Spirit both Israel and the heathen might receive the light of God.

In moving this resolution Mr. Arthur referred to the loneliness of many a missionary, to whom he trusted the message of the Conference would bring encouragement. He believed that the movement towards Christian union had been largely stimulated through the coming together of Christians for missionary effort.

Immediately after the creation of the Evangelical Alliance its missionary contacts began to appear. The very first volume of the Alliance magazine, issued in 1847, contains a significant letter from Hongkong.

CHINA

China was then only just opening her doors to the foreigner. After centuries of seclusion, she had agreed in 1842 lo the opening of five ports, the chief of which, Hongkong, was ceded to Britain. At once the light of the Gospel shone out in Hongkong, and the letter from that city to the newly-born "Alliance" tells of the coming to Hongkong, from the distant city of Shiklung, of a group of people who were already being drawn towards Christ. They brought with them a letter to explain their coming. "We feel indebted," they said, "in the highest degree to the grace and mercy of God that Pia and Hiemlang" (two converts) "presented us with the sacred books and have acquainted us with the truth as it is in Jesus, whereby our ignorance has been removed. It was therefore not too much for us to make a journey of 1,000 li [500 km], hoping that you, teacher, will instruct us morning and evening. We repent heartily of our sins, and wish to become soon disciples of Christ."

Such a letter must have confirmed and quickened the missionary zeal of the infant Alliance.

INDIA: DR. DUFF

In 1852 came a communication from Dr. Alexander Duff, the great educational pioneer in India, who had taken up the torch of missionary leadership from the hands of the dying Carey. Duff wrote, asking to be received into the Alliance, respecting which he said: "To the doctrines which constitute its basis I subscribe with my whole heart, and of its spirit and objects I entirely approve." He suggested that he should be enrolled as "one of the Calcutta correspondents of the Alliance".

One can imagine the pleasure with which Dr. Duff would be welcomed into the Alliance.

TURKEY

After China and India, Turkey and the Moslem realm! In 1855 a grant of £100 by the Alliance Committee for evangelistic work in Armenia elicited a letter from Constantinople, telling of opening opportunities "Signs of awakening and advance appear in every direction.... We live in exciting times. Great events are doubtless just before us in the world's career."

This was so indeed, for it was the time of the Crimean War, when the gates of the Middle East were opening towards great lands of the far East and South.

THE LUDHIANA CALL

In 1860 an event in the mission field brought to the Evangelical Alliance a greatly-widened influence. A group of missionaries in Ludhiana, North-West India, had been accustomed to issue a call of their own to united prayer, and now they sent to the Alliance a proposal for the linking of this with that of the Alliance, and an appeal that the Alliance Call to Prayer which had been issued to a limited circle might now be sent out to every part of the world. To this the Executive gladly agreed and so the Week became the *"Universal* Week of Prayer".

THE SPELL OF THE LORD JESUS

As years passed, many incidents from the mission field lit up the records of the Alliance. In 1873 two events in widely-sundered regions illustrated the love and devotion called forth by Him whom both the Alliance and the missionaries delight to proclaim. In Ceylon a girl of a high-caste family lay dying. For years her family had tried to seclude her from the influence of the Christians who had won her heart for Christ in a mission school. Now her father came to her bedside and said: "This is your last hour; call on Cadaswamy and Kathuavale (Tamil gods) for help." "No," she replied, "I've Jesus with me – the Lord Jesus." And with this confession on her lips she passed away to be for ever with the Lord.

In the same year David Livingstone died, kneeling in prayer by his bed in Central Africa, and leaving behind him this written testimony: "My own Jesus, my King, my Life, my All. I have given, I dedicate my whole self to Thee. Accept me, O gracious Father, and grant that ere this year has gone I may finish my task. In Jesus' name I ask it. Amen." The great African missionary and the Ceylonese girl were one in their passionate devotion to Jesus. He was their secret – for holy life and victorious death.

A MISSIONARY FAREWELL

In 1878 the Alliance recorded a memorable missionary meeting held in the Metropolitan Tabernacle, London. C. H. Spurgeon was in the chair and a party of ex-slaves took farewell of English friends before leaving for Africa, for the evangelisation of their race. The chief speaker of the evening. was the venerable Robert Moffat, who spoke of his long years in Africa and of his love for its people. He had told degraded savages of the Saviour and had witnessed the transforming of their lives.

A BISHOP'S SURPRISE

The same volume of *Evangelical Christendom* told of the arrival of Grenfell and Comber at San Salvador, and of a London Missionary Society party at Lake Tanganyika. It gave also the testimony of Bishop Wiley, of the American Episcopal Church, who told of the disappointment with which he had left China twenty-five years before, after a season of apparently fruitless labour. Now he had gone back and found the spiritual harvest of those years of sowing. Where he left five preachers there were now 511, and he could take a long journey across China and stop every night at a mission station with a Christian family.

The Alliance magazine has thus continually given surveys of missions, presenting a panoramic view of the progress of missionary effort in many fields.

When Dr. Zwemer, the great missionary authority on Islam, visited London in 1922, *Evangelical Christendom* paid a warm tribute to him and to the British and Foreign Bible Society, which it described as "the pioneer of missionary work wherever men can read the translated word". Dr. Zwemer was optimistic on the future of missions to Moslems, feeling that the Bible had created a new atmosphere and moral sense among the Mohammedans.

A CONGO INCIDENT

A touching and beautiful story from the Congo was told at an Evangelical Alliance meeting by Dr. J. R. Temple, of the Bible House. At one of the stations of the Baptist Missionary Society on that river the missionary sought by the exhibition of a film of our Lord's life to bring the Gospel home to an illiterate people. Crowds gathered and among them a young man was wheeled near on a hospital bed. The pictures showed the wonderful story from the manger of Bethlehem to the Passion. At length our Lord was seen, weary and burdened under His Cross and falling beneath it. The young man sprang from the hospital bed and was making his way towards the screen. "You cannot do that," cried the doctor, "get back." The patient replied, "I only wanted to help Him to carry His cross."

Surely that is the appeal that the story of the Saviour's love makes in every land to the sensitive heart. The Evangelical Alliance seeks, by making known things on the mission field that are "lovely and of good report", to promote the missionary spirit.

A GREAT INDIAN WOMAN

The death of Pandita Ramabai called forth from the Alliance magazine a glowing tribute to her work for India. Endowed with a retentive memory and a gift for languages, she early became learned. As a young widow she visited England and gave herself to Christ. She now felt she had a mission to her sisters. "She founded a school", says *Evangelical Christendom*, "where hundreds of girls were educated. Widows, deserted wives and famine victims won her sympathy and help. Her school grew into a regular colony with some thousand to two thousand members. . . . Her life was God-given and she relied on God for the maintenance of her many-sided activities. Her Mukti Colony is unique in India."

MISSIONARY REUNIONS – THE UGANDA CATHEDRAL

The missionary interest of the Alliance has also been shown in the holding of Missionary Reunions in the London headquarters. In these, Christian leaders of many Churches have met missionaries from numerous fields and the unity of the home and overseas work has been realised and strengthened. At one of these reunions the Bishop of Uganda was the guest speaker and the occasion was described in her graphic way by "Lorna", of the *British Weekly*. She told of the pleasant reception-rooms overlooking the garden of Russell Square, and of the friends who crowded them, while late comers sat on the stairs. She pictured the tall, dignified figure of the Bishop as he spoke of the changes in Uganda and of the progress of Christianity among the people, marked by the noble cathedral at Kampala. "We have a link," he said, "with your Alliance and its Week of Prayer, for our people come by hundreds, often after long, exhausting days of work, that they may pray in their c athedral."

CENTRAL AMERICA – LOST CIVILISATION

At another reunion Mr. Kenneth Grubb told of the evangelisation of Central America, and especially of the Presbyterian work in Guatemala. Here is an Indian population living between volcanoes and accustomed to pour out votive offerings to the gods of fire. They represent an ancient civilisation which has left behind it pyramids and ruins of palaces and temples. Today, said Mr. Grubb, there is among them a great response to the Gospel. In Guatemala there are about 600 centres where groups of Christians meet. Many of these have been started through the visits of country people to market-towns where they bought copies of the Bible which they carried back to their villages. Around these, little Bible-reading groups gathered, who sought the help of missionaries and became Christian fellowships.

THE LUDHIANA COLLEGE

On another occasion, a lady speaker, Miss C. Tiling, told of her visit to Ludhiana, already so intimately connected with the history of the Alliance. With the help of lantern views taken by herself, she described the famous Women's Christian Medical College there, with which Dame Edith Brown has been so honourably associated from the first. A pleasant outcome of this meeting was the gift of £150 to this valuable work from two sisters who were present.

INDIAN OUTCASTES

At another reunion, Dr. Wilson Cash, now Bishop of Worcester, spoke of the work in India among the sixty million outcastes, and quoted the words of Dr. Ambedkar, the outcaste leader, who in speaking to a mass meeting of his people said that Hinduism could no longer help them and the time had come when they must change their faith. It is good to know that many of them have lately turned to Christ.

JEWS IN ROMANIA

While most of these reunions have had to do with missions to the heathen, God's ancient people have not been overlooked', and at one meeting Rev. J. H. Adeney gave a review of work among Jews in Romania, where, besides the Gospel services for adults, schools for 500 or 600 Jewish children were being carried on.

A KING'S LETTER

A bright side-light on missionary success is given in the Alliance record of a Church Missionary meeting in Queen's Hall, at which Archdeacon Kitching, of Uganda, spoke. He recalled the cruel deeds of King Mwanga, who caused three of his pages who had become Christians to be slowly burned to death. The Archdeacon, standing before his Queen's Hall audience, drew from his pocket a small sheet of paper which contained a letter from the present King – Mwanga's son – written to congratulate the Archdeacon on his nomination as Bishop. The young King had been a Christian from his childhood, an earnest promoter of the faith his father had persecuted.

A change so dramatic showed vividly the transforming power of the Gospel, and the meeting was thrilled by the episode.

THE TAMBARAM CONFERENCE

The important missionary Conference, representing sixty-four nations, held at Tambaram (India) in December, 1938, awakened the keen interest of the World's Evangelical Alliance. This was shown, first, in the inclusion of the Conference among the topics for prayer during the Universal Week of Prayer, in 1938. Then, in preparation for the event, the Alliance magazine published a statement pointing out the special significance of the Conference, in which it was planned that the representatives of the "Younger Churches" should, for the first time in such assemblies, actually exceed in number those from the "Older" ones. This in itself was an indication of the success the Missionary Movement had already won.

When, at length, the Conference was sitting, the Alliance Council sent it a message of warm greeting, with the assurance of prayer that under the guidance of the Holy Spirit the Conference might help to foster the unity of the Spirit and give a new impetus to the work of evangelisation.

A grateful reply came from Tambaram, signed by J. R. Mott, the President of the Conference. This stated that the Alliance message had added to the sense of world-wide fellowship enjoyed by the Conference and had contributed "a vital part" to the result of the meeting which had transcended the highest expectations.

MISSIONS AND THE CALL TO THE UNIVERSAL WEEK OF PRAYER

In closing this account of the co-operation of the Evangelical Alliance in Missions, it is pleasant to recall the letter sent out annually by the Alliance to announce the Universal Week of Prayer. In this letter the secretaries of the great missionary societies, by invitation of the Alliance, join with Bishops, Presidents and Moderators of the various Churches in appealing for the observance in every land of this sacred Week.

CHAPTER XIII

CELEBRATIONS MARKING HISTORY, 1896–1946

IN an earlier chapter (IV) the historic celebrations of the Alliance during its first half-century were described, culminating in the Jubilee gathering in London. We have now to tell of the celebrations of the second fifty years.

THE THIRTEENTH INTERNATIONAL CONFERENCE AND DIAMOND JUBILEE OF ALLIANCE

In 1907 the Diamond Jubilee of the Alliance was celebrated in London by international gatherings held in the King's Hall, Holborn. At the opening meeting Lord Kinnaird presided, and addresses were delivered by Bishop Handley Moule (of Durham), Dr. G. S. Barrett (Norwich) and the representatives of many countries. The speaker from Korea told of a great work proceeding there: "A few weeks ago," he said, "I preached a sermon in the city of Paning before an audience of Christian Koreans, in a place where the average attendance at the Sunday morning service was larger than this audience." Bishop Hartzell told of great things taking place in Africa, and Mr. Stark described South America as sealed by martyrs' blood – in the North by that of the Moravians, in Brazil by that of the Huguenots, and in the cold islands of Tierra del Fuego by that of Captain Allen Gardiner.

During the following days valuable addresses were delivered by Dean Wace (of Canterbury) on "Evangelical Religion and Roman Catholicism", and by Bishop Cabrera (of Spain), Pastor Christlieb (of Germany), Baron Nicolai (of Russia), Pastor R. Saillens (of Paris) and many others on different aspects of Evangelical belief and progress. The proceedings were pleasantly varied by social intercourse, one day at the British and Foreign Bible Society's House, and another at Trent Park, New Barnet, the residence of Mr. F. A. Bevan.

CORONATION OF KING GEORGE V, 1911

As the time of the Coronation approached, the Alliance Executive addressed an appeal "To Our Friends and Brethren in Christ Jesus throughout the United Kingdom and the British Empire" for prayer on behalf of the King and Queen and Nation.

The sequel was great. In London central gatherings, attended by crowds, were held in Queen's Hall, while numerous other meetings took place in the suburbs. Throughout the Provinces also, and indeed throughout the Empire, remarkable demonstrations betokened the spirit of loyalty and of prayerful concern for the reign of King George and his gracious consort Queen Mary.

SEVENTIETH ANNIVERSARY OF ALLIANCE

The Seventieth Anniversary of the Alliance was held in 1916. The assembly met in the Mansion House, by invitation of the Lord Mayor of London (Sir Charles Wakefield). The beautiful Egyptian Hall was crowded when the Lord Mayor took the chair, supported by many religious leaders. It was in time of war, yet an enthusiastic spirit prevailed, for all were gathered under the banner of the Prince of Peace, whose coming triumph is the hope of every Christian heart.

Memorable speeches were given by Lord Kinnaird, Prebendary Webb-Peploe and the Rev. R. C. Gillie. Emphasis was laid on the fourfold objective of the Alliance – Christian unity, religious liberty, prayer and evangelism.

400TH ANNIVERSARY OF REFORMATION (LUTHER'S THESES)

In 1917, gatherings were held at Queen's Hall to commemorate the birth of the Reformation, dated from October 31, 1517, when Luther nailed his ninety-five theses to the door of the Castle Church of Wittenberg. Inspiring addresses on the great Reformation doctrines were delivered by Dean Wace (Canterbury), the Rev. W. Fuller Gooch (Norwood), Principal Selbie (Oxford) and Prof. Carnegie Simpson (Cambridge).

SUPPORT OF THE LEAGUE OF NATIONS

In 1920 the Alliance called a meeting at Queen's Hall in support of the League of Nations. This league was then a political hope, but many felt it was failing. As Sir Donald Maclean said: "Spiritual forces alone can lift the League of Nations out of the rut into which it has at present fallen." This meeting was an attempt to show that it could be lifted. The chair was taken by Lord Robert Cecil, and addresses were given by Sir Donald Maclean, Dr. W. T. A. Barber (President of the Wesleyan Conference), and the Rev. D. C. Macgregor (Moderator of the Presbyterian Assembly). The gathering constituted a call to the Churches to bring to the League that spiritual purpose and faith which could alone make it a victorious and enduring factor in the life of the world.

THE REFORMATION MESSAGE FOR TODAY

In 1924 a meeting was called at Queen's Hall to sound the Reformation Message for Today. The chair was occupied by Sir William Joynson-Hicks, who asked: "What did the Reformation do?" and answered: (1) "It restored to us the Holy Scriptures; (2) It abolished Papal jurisdiction in this country; (3) It gave us a revitalised Church and Nation." Dr. W. Y. Fullerton followed with another question: "What was the truth Luther brought to us?" His answer was: "(1) The just shall live by faith; (2) The efficacy of Grace; (3) The Open Mind." Sir Thomas Inskip spoke of our need to recover the *spirit* of those who suffered and died for their faith in Reformation days; and Dr. J. D. Jones (Bournemouth) dealt with the Open Bible and the Open Mind.

EIGHTIETH ANNIVERSARY OF ALLIANCE (BEGINNING)

In June, 1926, was held the celebration of the opening of the Eightieth Anniversary of the Alliance. In the afternoon of June 10th a large gathering met in the King's Hall, Holborn. Mr. R. C. Hart-Dyke, Chairman and Treasurer of the Alliance, presided, and inspiring addresses were given by the Rev.

Thomas Nightingale (Secretary of the National Free Church Council) and the Rev. John McNeill.

In the evening, Bishop Taylor-Smith presided, and the speakers were the Rev. H. Elvet Lewis, the poet-preacher, and Mr. McNeill again, speaking with characteristic wit and spiritual fervour.

80TH ANNIVERSARY OF ALLIANCE (COMPLETION OF YEAR)

The further celebration of the eightieth year of the Alliance took place in June, 1927. The meetings were preceded by a Sunday service in Wesley's Chapel, City Road, London, at which Dr. W.Y. Fullerton preached a sermon entitled "Where is the Alliance?" the theme being suggested by the enquiry of the two Persians who in 1861 came to London to seek the aid of the Alliance in obtaining religious liberty for their land.

On the following day the foreign delegates to the Conference were entertained to luncheon in the Connaught Rooms, built on the site of the Freemasons' Hall, in which the Alliance was inaugurated. Mr. R. C. Hart-Dyke presided and spoke of the associations of the place, especially welcoming the presence of Mr. and Mrs. Thomas Leigh, of Liverpool, the city in which the preparatory Conference of 1945 had been held. The Chairman also named with honour several of the guests from abroad – Señor Fernando Cabrera (Spain), Pastor Janni (Italy), Herr Nagel (Germany), Professor Hamaradka (Czechoslovakia), Dr. Stegegna (Holland), Pastor Hoyois (Belgium), Mr. Adam Padin (Estonia), Pastor Helenius (Finland), and M. C. Merle D'Aubigné (France).

In the evening a Thanksgiving Meeting was held in the King's Hall, Holbom. At this the Right Hon. Sir William Joynson-Hicks (Home Secretary) took the chair. M. Merle D'Aubigné was the first speaker and related an incident which he had learned in Warsaw. Before a large church in that city stood a great statue of Christ bearing His cross, with a light on either side burning night and day. Years ago a Jewish boy passed. He had been told when he passed a church to spit on the ground and utter a curse on the name of Jesus. But that day the boy saw a poor woman prostrate on the pavement, borne down by grief and misery; then the woman looked up and caught sight of the figure of Jesus carrying His Cross. She stood up, relieved, and said: "Now I feel better." The boy thought that, after all, there might be something in the Saviour of the Christians. This started thoughts that, after years, drew him to Christ.

Pastor Janni, minister of the Waldensian Church, San Remo, spoke of the movement of spiritual reform caused by the sending out of the "poor preachers of Lyons" four centuries before Luther; then of the persecution with fire and sword that drove the followers of Waldo to the Waldensian valleys, which thus became "the entrenched camps of religious liberty". "So," said Signor Janni, "came into being the historic Italian Evangelical Church." The speaker went on to express the indebtedness of his Church to the Evangelical Alliance for its influence on behalf of religious liberty.

Herr Nagel spoke of the influence of the Alliance in Germany, referring to Conferences held annually in various States, and especially to that in Blankenburg, from the meetings in which a stream of blessing went out into the spiritual life of Germany. Senor Cabrera touched the meeting with his story of the sufferings of Protestant martyrs in Spain through the Inquisition, sufferings which, however, the Alliance had done much to alleviate and bring to an end. Dr. G. H. Hanson told of the missions which had sprung up as the result of the work of the Alliance in Canada, which he had recently visited in company with Archdeacon Madden, of Liverpool.

The later Conferences were diversified with some social functions; one day the foreign delegates being motored to Oxford, where they visited the Bodleian Library, some of the Colleges and the spot where Ridley and Latimer were burned; and another day a Garden Party being held in Russell Square, opposite the Alliance headquarters.

BUNYAN TERCENTENARY

On November 22nd, 1928, a great meeting, organised by the Alliance, was held in Queen's Hall, to commemorate the birth of John Bunyan in 1628. Following the Chairman, Sir William Joynson-Hicks, addresses were delivered by the Archbishop of Canterbury (Dr. Lang) and the Rev. W.Y. Fullerton. The Archbishop, paying tribute to the genius of Bunyan and the charm of his great book, drew two lessons: (1) Each of us must make his own pilgrimage by help of divine grace; (2) Our civilisation is insecure unless it moves onwards toward the City of God. Dr. Fullerton asked three questions: (1) Do I believe there is a Celestial City? (2) Is sin to me an intolerable burden? (3) Am I sure my feet are in the pilgrim way?

Messages were received from the King and Prime Minister (Mr. Stanley Baldwin). The evening closed with dialogues and musical illustrations from the cantata "Bunyan the Dreamer", composed by the conductor, the Rev. Carey Bonner.

SILVER JUBILEE OF KING GEORGE V AND QUEEN MARY

On May 8th, 1935, a United Thanksgiving Service, to mark the Silver Jubilee of the King and Queen, was held, by arrangement of the Evangelical Alliance, in the Albert Hall, London. The great hall was filled with an audience drawn from every class. On either side of the organ was grouped a choir of 1,000. At a table draped with the Union Jack sat the Chairman, the Bishop of Norwich, supported by many religious leaders. After the National Anthem and the Chairman's opening speech, the Duke of Kent, who received an enthusiastic welcome, gave an address. Remarking on the warmth of the patriotic celebration, he said that, though the Albert Hall held 8,000 people, he understood that, had it been five times as great, it could have been filled. He quoted the King's declaration: "The foundations of national glory are set in the homes of the people", and paid a son's tribute to the beauty of the home life of the King and Queen. In closing, he read a telegram he had just received from Buckingham Palace: "I am glad to know that you are able to attend the meeting of the World's Evangelical Alliance, British Organisation, at the Albert Hall this evening. Please convey to all present my sincere thanks for their kind congratulations and good wishes on the occasion of my Silver Jubilee. – George R. and I."

Bishop Taylor Smith having led in prayer, Sir William Birdwood read the Scripture and the hymn "O God of Bethel" was sung, followed by the General Thanksgiving. The Master of the Rolls then spoke, referring to the twenty-five years' reign of "a great and good man – a great and good King".

After prayer by the Revs. W. Younger and R. C. Gillie, letters were read from the Prince of Wales and the Prime Minister, and a collection, amounting to £261, was taken for King George's Jubilee Trust. The last address was by Lord Bledisloe, retiring Governor-General of New Zealand, and the service culminated in the "Act of Homage", an Empire call to Thanksgiving and Prayer, in the words of which the vast audience reverently joined.

After the Doxology the choir gave a magnificent rendering of the "Hallelujah Chorus" and, with the fervent repetition of the National Anthem, this memorable service closed.

NINETIETH ANNIVERSARY OF THE ALLIANCE

The Ninetieth Anniversary of the Alliance was celebrated in 1936, in King's Hall, Holborn, under the presidency of Mr. Andrew Williamson. The first speaker was the Rev. the Hon. W. Talbot Rice, Hon. Secretary of the Alliance, who commended to the audience St. Augustine's creed:

> "A whole Christ for my Salvation,
> A whole Bible for my Staff,
> A whole Church for my Fellowship,
> A whole world for my Parish."

Addresses followed by Dr. J. W. Ewing and the Rev. E. J. T. Bagnall.

A conversazione ensued, by invitation of Mr. and Mrs. Williamson. A surprise came to the guests when a birthday cake blazing with the light of ninety candles was wheeled in on a trolley and after being cut by the hostess was made available for all present to share, while wishing the Alliance "Many happy returns of the day".

At the evening meeting the Bishop of Norwich presided and an address was given by Mr. A. R. Wise, M.P., on "Christianity and Foreign Affairs".

JUBILEE OF BLANKENBURG CONFERENCE

In the same year the Jubilee or the Blankenburg Conference, organised by the German branch of the Alliance, was celebrated. This Conference is held in a beautiful region of Thuringia, "the Green Heart of Germany". It began in 1886 in the home of a Christian lady, Fraulein von Weling, who invited a few friends, among whom was Dr. Baedeker of the Evangelical Alliance Council, to come together for spiritual fellowship. Only eight responded, but a living movement had been started which grew year by year. It was based on the principles of the Alliance, whose leaders were speakers at the gatherings. Dr. F. B. Meyer, who was a frequent speaker, paid a gracious tribute in the Alliance organ to Fraulein von Weling, telling of the hospitality with which she would provide for as many as 800 guests at Convention time, no payment being received except such gifts as guests liked to place in a little box by the door. She told Dr. Meyer that the amounts were always sufficient, for God provided for her need. Fraulein von Weling died in 1900; the year before she had provided for some 1,200 persons, chiefly members of the Evangelical Alliance, who had come from England, France, Russia, Germany, Italy and other lands.

At the Jubilee celebration in 1936 the speakers from the British Organisation of the Alliance were Bishop Taylor Smith, the Rev. J. Chalmers Lyon, and Mr. H. M. Gooch. They were deeply impressed by the meetings which found their climax in the official celebration, for which the Burgomaster of the town granted the use of the Stadthalle, where 5,000 people listened to addresses by Professor Karl Heim and the British delegates.

The central theme of the gatherings was "We beheld His glory", and, as Mr. Lyon reported, "the sense of the presence and power of God was mightily manifested day after day".

WILLIAM TYNDALE – 400TH ANNIVERSARY OF DEATH

In the same year, 1936, the Alliance signalised the fourth centenary of Tyndale's death by publishing a sketch of his life and work from the pen of the Rt. Hon. Isaac Foot. In this sketch Mr. Foot told the story of the Oxford graduate who, having come to know Christ as Saviour, gave himself to the task of rendering the New Testament into English, at a time when England was under the shadow of Romanist repression. Mr. Foot quotes a French writer who asked, "What is a great life?" and answered, "A purpose of youth fulfilled in riper age".

Mr. Foot shows that Tyndale's purpose of youth was to be fulfilled in persecution, exile, imprisonment, and finally a cruel death, but it was fulfilled, and Tyndale left to England the priceless legacy of the English New Testament, beside several books of the Old Testament. Well did John Foxe call him an "Apostle of England".

Mr. Foot's sketch was afterwards published by the Alliance as a booklet and had a wide circulation.

CORONATION OF KING GEORGE VI AND QUEEN ELIZABETH

On May 10th, 1937, the day before the Coronation of their Majesties, three great gatherings, called together by the Evangelical Alliance, met in Queen's Hall to seek the blessing of God upon King and Queen and Nation. The Bishop of Norwich presided at the morning meeting, at which the first speaker was H.R.H. the Duke of Kent, who was accompanied on the platform by the Duchess. The Duke reminded the audience that the Coronation was no mere pageantry. "It is," he said, "a religious ceremony of the very deepest significance. I have been on many journeys that have taken me to the furthest corners of the Empire, and I know the closeness of the links which hold the Empire together, and really they are sacred and family links, bound up with God and King and Home."

The words of the Duke and the presence of the Duchess and himself were a happy reminder of the unity between the Royal House and the nation in the deep fellowship of the hour. Other speakers were the Marquess of Crewe, General Sir Ian Hamilton and Dr. Campbell Morgan.

At the afternoon gathering the Bishop of London occupied the chair, and the speakers were Sir Thomas Inskip, Dr. Lamont (Moderator of the Church of Scotland) and the General Secretary of the Alliance. At the evening meeting

Sir Josiah Stamp presided and addresses were given by the Rev. M. E. Aubrey (Moderator of the Federal Council of the Evangelical Free Churches) and Gipsy Smith. The day closed with a spiritual appeal for the surrender of love and life to the King of kings.

FOURTH CENTENARY OF THE REFORMATION AND THE ENGLISH BIBLE

On June 28th, 1938, the 400th Anniversary of the issue of the Injunctions of 1538 ordering that a copy of the Bible in English should be set up in every Parish Church in England, was celebrated by the Evangelical Alliance in a National Thanksgiving Meeting in Queen's Hall. The Bishop of Norwich presided over a crowded audience, the service of praise being led by a large, united choir, conducted by Dr. J. E. Green, with Mr. Allan Brown at the organ.

Professor Ernest Barker referred to the two great bodies of English Christianity, Anglicanism and Nonconformity, both of which were founded on the Bible and found in it their deep unity. Sir Thomas Inskip spoke of the Bible and of the glory which broke forth from it upon the English people. Dr. S. M. Berry discussed the influence of the Bible on literature.

Thus on this occasion, as on many others during the century, the World's Evangelical Alliance has provided the public with a platform for the recall of an historic event and the consideration of its meaning for the living hour.

CHAPTER XIV

"EVANGELICAL CHRISTENDOM"

WHEN the Alliance was founded in 1846 it was resolved to start a magazine to promote its interests. This was done and in January, 1847, the first number of *Evangelical Christendom* appeared. Financial responsibility was assumed by a group of gentlemen who became proprietors, and editorial responsibility by another group.

In the opening number the Editors state their purpose to exalt the great, common truths which underlie the various Evangelical Communions, and in doing this they claim that they will have two special advantages. First, their articles will be contributed by scholars and theologians of all Churches and all countries (indeed, they had already promises from some of the ablest writers in Europe and America): and, second, the magazine would be suitable for circulation, not in a single denomination only, but in all.

In conclusion, "they cast themselves on the candour of their Christian brethren and still more upon the aids of celestial grace".

The address is signed by T. R. Birks, W. Chalmers, W. M. Bunting, J. Harris and Edward Steane. The magazine came out monthly and showed itself at once to be a full and comprehensive review of its subject: its first annual volume proved to be a book of 400 pages, while some of the later volumes ran to 600 and 700 pages.

SOME THEMES

The promise of the Editors was fulfilled from the first in the issue of a series of papers by prominent men on important themes. In the first volume were essays on "Apostolical Succession"; "The Communion of Saints"; "The Employment of Medical Men as Missionaries"; "Science and Literature considered in their bearings upon Divine Truth"; and "The Evangelical Alliance, its Great Object and Prayer as the Means of its Attainment". The naming of these specimen papers revealed the germ of movements which were to become familiar, such as Medical Missions and the Universal Week of Prayer.

BIOGRAPHIES

Another feature of *Evangelical Christendom* has from the beginning been its biographical sketches. In the 1847 volume there are two such sketches of special interest. The one brings before us the famous Swiss writer, Alexander Vinet.

A. VINET

Vinet, born at Lausanne in 1797, was a man of brilliant gifts. At the age of twenty-two he was invited to Basle and there appointed Professor of the French language and literature, while about the same time he was ordained to the ministry of the Gospel. At Basle he became famous as a writer on Christian themes, and in 1837 he was recalled to his own University at Lausanne to take the chair of Sacred Eloquence and Practical Theology. In 1845 the Free Church was formed there: he joined it and in the persecution which followed he lost his professorship. He still wrote books, but his health failed and he died in 1847. Probably his best-known work is his *Vital Christianity*, in which, after describing the glory of the Christian faith, he closes by saying "That which remained concealed from philosophers and sages, and most brilliant periods of the human intellect, twelve poor fishermen from the Lake of Judea quitted their nets to announce to the world".

THOMAS CHALMERS

The other sketch is of one of the most famous of Christian ministers – Thomas Chalmers. The writer of the sketch, in introducing it, says of his death: "Sure we are, that without one dissentient voice, Evangelical Christendom will acknowledge that its brightest luminary has set." Chalmers was born in Fifeshire in 1780. He studied at St. Andrews, but made no mark till he took up mathematics. Science now became his great interest, though at the age of twenty he was licensed to preach the Gospel and in 1803 settled in the pastoral charge of Kilmany. He still gave himself chiefly to mathematical study, as he in later years sadly confessed: "Strangely blinded that I was! What, Sir, is the object of mathematical science? Magnitude, and the proportions of magnitude. But then, Sir, I had forgotten two magnitudes. I thought not of the littleness of time, I recklessly thought not of the greatness of eternity."

Largely through the reading of William Wilberforce's *Practical View of Christianity*, Chalmers discovered the secret of Evangelical faith and became a humble believer in Jesus Christ as his Saviour. Now his lips were touched as with a live coal from the altar and his native eloquence blazed forth with a purer flame as he preached Christ and His Cross. In his Glasgow charge his sermons became renowned, while he laboured untiringly on behalf of the poor of the city. After eight years of this service he was called to professorial work, first at St. Andrews and then at Edinburgh University. At the Disruption in 1843 he led the newly-formed Free Church, and when the movement arose for the founding of the Evangelical Alliance he threw himself into it whole-heartedly, writing a pamphlet upon it just before the inaugural meeting of 1846. He pleaded specially for the Alliance to do some definite work, which as we know it did. He died suddenly in May, 1847, leaving a name famous for genius, character, and a ministry at once evangelical and philanthropic.

These early biographies have been followed in the magazine by many others all down the century.

BOOKS

Another feature of *Evangelical Christendom* from the first has been its discussion of valuable books. In the 1847 volume we find notices, among others, of McCheyne's *Remains*, McCrie's *Sketches of Scottish Church History*, *Vie de Henri Martyn*, *The Protector* by J. H. Merle D'Aubigné (the historian of the Reformation), and Macfarlane's *Revivals of the Eighteenth Century*; beside works dealing directly with the Alliance, such as Bickersteth's *Brief View of the Evangelical Alliance*, Massie's *Evangelical Alliance; its Origin and Development*, and the Report of the Conference at Freemasons' Hall, this last giving the reporters' minutes day by day of the proceedings of the inaugurating assembly.

The books noticed, and in many cases critically appraised, have amounted to many hundreds and constitute an interesting contribution to the history of religious literature during the hundred years. Some of the books thus treated, like *Essays and Reviews* and Newman's *Apologia*, represent standpoints not that of the Alliance, but they have their place in the record, and their contents are carefully and fairly considered.

THE ALLIANCE'S OWN STORY

The central line of the magazine is naturally the unfolding of the Alliance's own story, and in its pages we see the monthly meetings of the Executive Council and hear the leaders initiating policy or planning movements; we are carried on to Conferences in great cities of the world; we watch the rise of men destined to fame, or mourn with their contemporaries the passing of men whose names to this day are household words. Sometimes we hear the clash of differing opinions, for the Alliance has never been a colourless unity, in which all said the same things. Dr. Stoughton, one of the founders, said even of that wonderful first Conference, "Our Alliance was cradled in controversy". But there has been the deep harmony of men who from many schools found themselves one in things sacred and essential.

RELIGIOUS CONDITIONS THROUGHOUT THE WORLD

The wide outlook of the Alliance has been shown all along in the reports of religious conditions in many lands given in its magazine.

FRANCE

In the 1847 volume we have a graphic account of the position of Christianity in Europe, from the pen of Dr. R.

Baird, of New York. In speaking of France he makes the significant statement that "The clear enunciation of the Gospel takes the French Catholic by surprise. How often have I heard men say to me, when I explained the Gospel as understood by Protestants, 'And is this Christianity? We had no conception of any other Christianity than that which we saw in our churches and in the ceremonies practised there'".

No doubt these words have continued to tell the truth all through the hundred years.

SOUTH AMERICA

A series of seven communications occurs in the same volume from Dr. James Thomson, telling of the religious position in the various countries of South America. The writer speaks of the religion everywhere prevailing as Roman Catholic and of a specially low type, which be attributes to the mixture of races, European colonisers having married natives, who were in many cases not weaned from heathenism.

RUSSIAN "MILK-EATERS"

In the next volume (1848) an interesting article occurs, signed T.B.K., in which is described a visit to a Russian community bearing the strange name of "Molokaners", or "Milk-eaters". This was a sect which had separated from the Russian Church on account of the invocations of saints, the various masses, the worship of pictures and relics and similar observances insisted on by the Russian Church. Their name "Milk-eaters" bad been given them, perhaps in derision, like our "Teetotallers", because most of them drank no fermented liquor. They had been subjected to severe persecution and at last the Russian Government had banished them as a community to the remote district of Grusia. Here they settled quietly and others in sympathy with their religious position joined them until in that wild region they had sixty to eighty villages containing thousands of families. The rule of their faith was the Bible, of which they possessed an extraordinary knowledge. Where there was no school, the children were instructed by their parents, with a special emphasis on

Scripture. They cherished the expectation of our Lord's speedy return.

RELIGIOUS LIBERTY

A prominent feature of *Evangelical Christendom* through all the years has been its advocacy of religious freedom and its care for the persecuted. Of this many examples have been given in the chapter (VIII) devoted to this subject. A poem at once touching and inspiring is quoted in the 1847 volume, entitled "The Christian Captive's Welcome To Death". It was written at the close of a long and terrible imprisonment and under sentence of death at the stake, by Francisco Sen Roman, or Burgos, one of the earliest Spanish martyrs, A.D. 1544. The following lines form a part of it.

> "It is told me I must die,
>   O happy news!
> Be glad, O my soul,
>   And rejoice in Jesus, thy Saviour.
>
> It is told me I must die,
>   O happy news!
> I shall be freed from misery,
> I shall no more suffer pain;
> I shall no more be subject to sin.
>
> It is told me I must die,
>   O what happiness!
>   I am going
> To the place of my rest,
> To the land of the living,
> To the haven of security,
> To the kingdom of peace,
> To the palace of my God,
> To the nuptials of the Lamb,
> To sit at the table of my King,
> To feed on the bread of angels,
> To see what no eye hath seen,
> To hear what no ear hath heard,
> To enjoy what the heart of man cannot comprehend."

In the last verse the saint and martyr cries:

"O my Father,
Come now in mercy and receive Thy child;

— — — — —

And forgive all those who are guilty of His death."

By the recall of this last utterance of one about to pass beyond the persecutor's power, *Evangelical Christendom* in its first campaign sounded a trumpet-note to every age in defence of the freedom of the Christian soul.

LIGHT ON WORLD-EVENTS

As the years pass the pages of the magazine bring into clear light many a world-event which has its bearing on the Evangelical cause. I 1857 the Indian Mutiny is taking place and a letter from Poona tells of the death of Sir Henry Havelock and quotes a speech delivered by him at the formation of the Western India Organisation of the Evangelical Alliance, of which he became Vice-President. In this speech Havelock told Rowland Hill's story of the Angel Gabriel saying, in answer to an enquiry, that in Heaven they had no Romanists, Churchmen, Wesleyans, Presbyterians, Baptists or Independents; they had "none but those who fear God and work righteousness". This story, Havelock remarked, appeared to him "to contain within itself the whole pith and matter of the Evangelical Alliance".

ENLARGEMENT OF MAGAZINE

In 1860 the Editors announced the enlargement of the journal and the introduction of new features – articles on Scripture and theological literature by well-known scholars; others connected with the great missionary work, in which so many Churches had become engaged, such as reviews of philosophies and languages of the East, and essays on the Equipment of Oriental Missionaries. In this year the annual volume ran to 700 pages.

A MISSIONARY EVENT

In 1862 we find a record of the expulsion of J. G. Paton from the island of Tanna (in the New Hebrides). Paton had settled there, with two other missionaries, in 1858. The inhabitants, degraded and cruel in type, resolved to murder them. The missionaries barricaded their house for a time and then managed to escape into the bush. At length a sail appeared on the horizon and signals of distress brought a boat which rescued the missionaries. The work was checked but was not suffered to be closed. Paton returned, and faced innumerable dangers, but was conscious in the midst of them of the presence and protection of the Lord, and a great work was done. A strong church was built up on the island and men who had sought to kill the missionaries were brought to Christ and sat with them in communion at the Table of the Lord. The present writer remembers sitting with his fellow-students under the shade of the "Question Oak" in the grounds of C. H. Spurgeon and hearing the wonderful story from the lips of John G. Paton himself, then an old man with a crown of white hair and a face radiant with love to the Saviour.

In 1872 the magazine celebrated its Twenty-fifth Anniversary by changes to enhance its value and facilitate its circulation; and in the following year it united with another publication, *Christian Work; or The News of the Churches*.

THE BOXER MASSACRES

In 1900 the magazine reported with sorrow the Boxer massacres in China, when many missionaries won the martyr's crown and many native converts showed the effect of Christian teaching by voluntarily sharing the sufferings of their teachers. The Secretary of the Evangelical Alliance in Pekin told of the heroic choice of the Christian assistant, Li, dispenser in the L.M.S. hospital, who when told that he might go and save himself, "with a face as white as death", elected to remain. As of old, there were those who would not "accept deliverance that they might obtain a better resurrection".

W. Y. FULLERTON ON THE ALLLANCE

In 1915 the first World War was raging, but *Evangelical Christendom* was able to give an inspiring message in its report of Dr. Fullerton's address at an Alliance meeting. Quoting General Foch's telegram to General Joffre, "My left wing is being crushed, my right wing is being crushed, but I am hammering at the centre", Fullerton felt this to be a picture of the contest waged by those who bear Christ's name; the left wing, having adopted a vain philosophy, fails; the right wing, having hidden the truth in ceremonies, also fails. The Evangelical Alliance stands at the centre, where Christ is, with His Cross, and He will yet win the victory.

SOMERVELL AND LIDDELL

In 1924 *Evangelical Christendom* illustrates the broad human outlook of the Alliance, as it refers to two of the heroes of adventure and sport – Dr. Howard Somervell, of the Everest Expedition, who reached the great height of 28,000 feet and afterwards became a missionary, and Eric Liddell, the Olympic Games champion, who refused to run on Sunday and went instead to address a mission service in Paris. He also became a missionary.

SCOTTISH CHURCH UNION

In 1929 we have the record of the union of the Church of Scotland with the Free Church, celebrated in Edinburgh. The Council of the Alliance sent a letter of congratulation and commissioned the General Secretary to attend as its representative. Mr. Gooch describes in *Evangelical Christendom* the morning scene as, between crowded lines of witnesses, the processions of ministers from the two churches met in the street and the two Moderators grasped one another's hands and walked side by side to St. Giles' Cathedral. In the afternoon Mr. Gooch attended a public gathering of some 12,000 persons, among whom were the Duke and Duchess of York.

The consummation of the union was, in the words of the

Moderator, "a call to intensive evangelism", and the evening address of the Archbishop of Canterbury laid emphasis on "Christ and Christian Unity".

TRIBUTES TO THE BIBLE

One of the most valuable features of *Evangelical Christendom* through the years has been its witness to the value and sacredness of the Scriptures. In 1929 it welcomed Sir Flinders Petrie to Alliance House and after the distinguished archaeologist had told of his explorations in Egypt and Palestine confirming Bible history, a presentation from Alliance friends of £233 was made to him towards the expense of his work.

Sir Leonard Woolley has also been repeatedly heard at Alliance gatherings as he has told of his excavations at Ur of the Chaldees and other ancient cities, throwing light upon Abraham's period and even earlier times.

The magazine has also preserved valuable utterances, as, for example, the message of President Wilson to American soldiers in the earlier Great War, accompanying the gift of the New Testament: "The Bible is the Word of Life. I beg that you will read it. . . . When you have read the Bible you will know that it is the Word of God, because you will have found it the key to your own heart, your own happiness and your own duty."

Later, it gives the fine words of Generalissimo Chiang Kai-Shek when referring to his imprisonment in Sian: "From my captors I asked but one thing, a copy of the Bible. In my solitude I had ample opportunity for reading and meditation. The greatness and love of Christ burst upon me with new inspiration."

Wise counsel is given in the magazine by the Rev. J. Chalmers Lyon in his verses beginning: –

A Chapter a Day

"A chapter a day, there's no better way
   Of reading the Bible, a chapter a day.
It will help you to live, it will help you to pray;
   You'll find it a solace, a strength and a stay.
Get into the habit and start right away,
   To read from your Bible a chapter a day."

THE ALLIANCE AND THE YOUNG

The interest of the Alliance in Christian youth is evident in the report of its organ on the Jubilee Service of Christian Endeavour, held at the Albert Hall in 1931.

The chief speaker was the Duke of York, who dwelt on the importance of preserving the Christian Vision. "You, ladies and gentlemen," he said, "believe that it is your bounden duty to keep the ideals of Christianity well in the front in public and private life. Hold fast to that belief, act on it, and you will be giving to your fellow men and women the highest service in your power."

It was reported that while C.E. started fifty years ago with a membership of fifty-seven, it now numbered 4,000,000 members and 80,000 societies, throughout the world.

THE ALLIANCE AND THE MORAVIANS

In 1932 *Evangelical Christendom* recorded the Conference organised by the Dutch branch of the Alliance at Zeist, the charming Moravian settlement near Utrecht. The gatherings were held in the spacious Moravian church, close to the ancient castle, which was once the residence of Count Zinzendorf. The British Organisation was represented by its General Secretary, who afterwards reported upon the impressive atmosphere of the conference as its theme, "The Person and Work of Christ", was considered. The memory of Zinzendorf and the association of John Wesley with the Moravians at the time of his spiritual renewal gave a special tone to the assembly.

THE ALLIANCE AND THE JEWS

The care of the Alliance for the Jewish people is illustrated in a poem quoted in *Evangelical Christendom* in 1943.

"Pray for the Peace of Jerusalem"
by HORATIUS BONAR

"Forgotten! No, that cannot be!
All other names may pass away,
But thine, My Israel, shall remain
An everlasting memory.

Forgotten! No, that cannot be!
   Inscribed upon my palms thou art,
The name I gave in days of old
   Is graven still upon my heart.

Forgotten! No, that cannot be!
   Beloved of thy God art thou,
His crown for ever on thy head,
   His name for ever on thy brow.

Forgotten! No, that cannot be I
   Sun, moon and stars may cease to shine,
But thou shalt be remembered still,
   For thou art His, and He is thine."

A FORTY-TWO YEARS' EDITORSHIP

There is one other fact to be recorded respecting the *Evangelical Christendom*, and it is a remarkable one. The magazine has been edited, and edited with conspicuous success, during the last forty-two years by Mr. H. Martyn Gooch, the General Secretary.

It is probable that such a tenure of editorship has few parallels.

H. R. H. The Duke of Kent addressing the great meeting in the Royal Albert Hall in celebration of the Silver Jubilee of King George V's Accession to the Throne (see page 121)

(above) Waldensian Church House at Torre Pellice (Italy) and (below) Moderator and Members of Synod in procession to open proceedings (see page 133)

CHAPTER XV

INCORPORATION OF THE ALLIANCE
(British Organisation)

AT the time of the formation of the Evangelical Alliance the fellowship constituting it was governed by the rules passed by the founders without legal formality. In course of time, however, as the responsibilities of the British Organisation increased, it was felt to be necessary that legal incorporation should be acquired, qualifying for the holding of property and the regular administration of funds.

In 1912, therefore, a Memorandum and Articles of Association were drawn up and completed, incorporating "The World's Evangelical Alliance" (British Organisation) under the Companies (Consolidation) Act of 1908. As this incorporation opened a new era of Alliance life, it was felt by the leaders of the British Organisation that the time had come for a change to be made in the use of the doctrinal statement hitherto required from persons joining the Alliance. The basis formulated in 1846 was long and detailed, and it was now felt that a shorter and simpler statement would be welcomed. It was therefore agreed, and inserted in the Articles of Association, that the following statement should appear on every form of application for membership and its acceptance should be a sufficient qualification:

"All are welcomed as members of the World's Evangelical Alliance (British Organisation) who, acknowledging the Divine Inspiration, Authority and Sufficiency of the Holy Scriptures, believe in one God – the Father; the Son, the Lord Jesus Christ our God and Saviour, who died for our sins and rose again; and the Holy Spirit, by whom they desire to have fellowship with all who form the one Body of Christ."

While the above is the present basis of membership in general, the acceptance of the original and fuller basis is still required of members of the Executive Council.

CHAPTER XVI

THE HEADQUARTERS

FOR a short time after its formation the Alliance occupied rooms at Exeter Hall, but in November, 1847, removed to 7 Adam Street, Strand, which became known as Alliance House. This remained for many years the home of the Alliance, in which the Executive and Committees met and the secretarial work was carried on.

In 1854 a step forward was taken in the provision of a reading-room there, to serve as a convenient meeting-place for members of the Alliance resident in London or visiting it.

For sixty-five years, 7 Adam Street continued as the Alliance centre and became truly historic ground, but at length the growing work of the Alliance made a larger building necessary and in 1912 the Executive secured the lease of a very desirable house in Russell Square (No. 19), pleasantly situated by the garden of the Square with its grassy lawns and shady trees. Appeal was made for £5,000 for the purchase of the lease and for the redecoration and equipment of the house, and the generous response enabled all preparations to be made and the house to be taken into occupation at the end of 1912.

In the new year of 1913 the house was dedicated to the service of God, the spacious reception rooms being filled with friends of the Alliance. Lord Kinnaird presided and addresses were given by the Revs. R. C. Gillie and Dinsdale T. Young, and Mr. F. A. Bevan. Congratulations were received from Alliance branches in many lands, and guests from abroad were entertained to dinner in the Holborn Restaurant.

The Russell Square house continued for many years to be the scene of happy and influential gatherings and manifold work. In 1937, an epoch was marked, when the lease of the house was renewed and improvements and redecoration were carried out. It was felt fitting that a Rededication Service should be held, and this was done on April 20th, under the chairmanship of the Treasurer, Mr. R. C. Hart Dyke; the speakers being Dr. J. W. Ewing (President of the National Free Church Council) and the Rev. A. H. Wilkinson (Clerical Secretary of the Bible Society).

Not long, however, were the improved and convenient headquarters to be enjoyed. During the great war which began in September of 1939 the house suffered several times from enemy bombs. For a time the work was carried on, though under difficulties, but in 1944 an intense shock through enemy action occasioned such damage that this beautiful house had to be evacuated. Happily, all papers and records were preserved and temporary premises were secured in the vicinity, at 30 Bedford Place.

On November 8th, 1944, the temporary headquarters were dedicated. The Right Hon. Isaac Foot, the new Treasurer, presided and addresses were given by Mr. Foot and the General Secretary. Interest was aroused through the pointing out by the Secretary of valuable mementoes of 1846, which had come safely through all the vicissitudes of ninety-eight years, including those of two great wars. There was the Bible of Sir Culling Eardley, the first Chairman and Treasurer of the Alliance; the Queen Anne table used by the founders; and, hanging on the wall of the council-room a framed silk handkerchief, painted in 1846 to commemorate the founding of the Alliance, and showing around the communion-cup in the centre the portraits of many of the founders. In these could be recognised the features of many of the foremost ministers and laymen of the various branches of the Church of Christ of that day.

As if to link the present with the past, personally-signed portraits of their Majesties, King George and Queen Elizabeth, were also hanging on the walls of the chamber.

As the gathering dispersed, all were thankful that in its time of need the Alliance had been led to a temporary home, pending the provision of the headquarters of the future.

CHAPTER XVII

OFFICIALS AT THE CENTRE

IN every extensive enterprise much depends on workers at the centre, who, in proportion to their industry and organising power, contribute to the success of the movement. Theirs is the service not so much of the crowded assembly as of the quiet office. The Evangelical Alliance has been happy in the possession of a line of such officials, including some who have been prominent not only behind the scenes but on the great occasion also.

At the beginning of the Alliance the secretariat was entrusted to a group of honoured men – W. M. Bunting, J. Leifchild, E. Bickersteth, James Hamilton and Edward Steane, with Dr. Steane marked out as "Official Secretary, pro tem". Very soon the group gave place to the individual in the appointment of W. Bevan, who served acceptably till his retirement in 1849, when he was succeeded by J.P. Dobson. Mr. Dobson rendered good service for nine years, having the help, during a part of his term, of C. Jackson as Travelling Secretary, and of J. W. Lester in the general work. In 1859 J. Davis became General Secretary and rendered valuable service for nineteen years, paying visits to Continental branches, during one of which he had helpful interviews with the German Emperor and Empress, and with Prince Bismarck. Mr. Davis had, during a part of his time, colleagues in Major-General Barrows and H. Schmettau, the latter acting as Foreign Secretary.

Then followed the valuable secretariat of A. J. Arnold (1878–1898), the first year as assistant, and then as General Secretary. Mr. Arnold was a man of fine gifts, both as an organiser and as a speaker. His secretariat culminated in the great Jubilee celebrations in 1896, in which he presented the story of the fifty years. With him as a colleague during much of his term of office was Major-General Field, later General Sir John Field.

Mr. Arnold died in 1898, and after a brief interval in which help was given by H. R. T. Jackson, E. P. Field, the son of Sir John, was appointed and served from 1899 to 1904.

In 1904, Henry Martyn Gooch entered upon the secretariat which, happily, continues to this day. He is the son of the Rev. W. Fuller Gooch, who named him after the great missionary to India and Persia. His forty-two years of office have shown him to be richly equipped, as a worker, a speaker, an organiser, one who makes easy contacts with people of every class, a lover of the Evangelical Alliance, and, still more, of Christ and the Gospel.

Mr. Gooch's administration has been specially notable for two features – first, his organisation of great Evangelical demonstrations. In this connection he has shown true leadership, approaching premiers, archbishops and heads of denominations with proposals for action, and then making appeal to the people, with the result that he has brought about services of united prayer in St. Paul's Cathedral and great assemblies in the Albert Hall, Queen's Hall and Central Hall, in support of Evangelical and patriotic causes.

The other feature has been his visitation of other lands on the Alliance's behalf. In this he has followed in the steps of earlier Secretaries, but modern facilities of travel added to the far longer duration of his secretariat have furnished him with more numerous opportunities. Thus in his first few years he went to Russia, Finland, Sweden, Malta, Italy and Switzerland. Of the later journeys, I mention only a few of special interest.

In 1926 Mr. Gooch visited the Waldensian Synod at Torre Pellice, the ecclesiastical capital of the valleys. Here he was reminded of the sufferings of the persecuted Waldenses for whom Milton appealed to God in his immortal sonnet:

"Avenge, O Lord, Thy slaughtered saints whose bones
Lie scattered on the alpine mountains cold."

To the annual gatherings of this Synod, held in the midst of historic scenes, Mr. Gooch was invited as representing the World's Evangelical Alliance, to which the Waldensians felt they owed much. He found the meetings deeply impressive and was elected by the assembly to the Tavola (the governing council of the Synod), a symbol of membership of which was publicly presented to him by the Moderator. In this kindly way this martyr-Church testified to the comfort and help which had come to it through the Alliance.

In 1927 there was a comprehensive journey to North-Eastern Europe; visits being paid to Norway, Denmark and Sweden, in the last of which Mr. Gooch was the guest of Prince Bernadotte, whom he found to be "to the forefront in everything spiritual in Sweden"; then to Finland and Estonia, where, as on other occasions, he visited Adam Podin's work and addressed the students of the Baptist Seminary; then to Latvia, where he visited Riga and took part in a united service in Sion Church, marked by "the Alliance spirit". On returning from the Baltic Provinces he confessed that his visits to Estonia and Latvia had made him feel a desire to raise his hat whenever he met an Estonian or a Latvian. So rich was the spiritual experience of these who have suffered so intensely in these latest years.

1930 found the Secretary in Augsburg (Germany) to represent the Alliance at the 400th Anniversary of the Augsburg Confession, that landmark of the Reformation. At the central Festival Service, held in the Barfusser Church (former Chapel of the Barefoot Monks), Mr. Gooch presented the Evangelical Alliance address of congratulation.

Later in the same year came a visit to Zurich, to a Conference of the League for the Defence and Furtherance of Protestantism. The local memories of Zwingli gave poignancy to the gatherings, which began day by day at 8 a.m.

In 1931 Mr. Gooch visited Albania, described as "Europe's smallest kingdom". The journey to it was a roundabout one, as it meant going to Bari (near Brindisi) and there taking ship up the Adriatic to Durazzo; thence, as there was no railway in Albania, by car (ten hours) to Kortaha. Here he visited the mission schools carried on by American missionaries. The population he found to be a mixed one – Moslems, Orthodox, Roman Catholic and a few Protestants. All these religions were represented in the Sunday morning service he took in the School Hall. Mr. Gooch also spoke at a Prison Service, the prisoners being gathered in a courtyard. On other days he visited the towns of Elbasan and Tirana.

In 1936 the Secretary was accompanied to Germany and Poland by Bishop Taylor Smith and the Rev. J. Chalmers Lyon. In Germany they attended the Blankenburg Convention. Then, proceeding to Poland, they visited Lodz,

Wiecbork, Thorn, Cieszyn (on the border-line between Poland and Czechoslovakia) and Warsaw. In Poland memorable services were held, in which the visitors were graciously received by Bishop Bursche, of the Lutheran Church, who, sad to relate, was tortured and killed in the war a few years after.

In 1937 a visit was paid to Hungary, where, at Budapest, the Hungarian branch of the Alliance held an "Alliance-Keswick" Conference. Here the Revs. A. St. John Thorpe and E. L. Langston were with Mr. Gooch as delegates from England. During the period of the Conference services were held in Debrecen, where, in the Museum, Munkacsy's famous picture "Ecce Homo" was seen. The picture furnished an illustration for an address to the pupils in the Reformed Church Seminary at Miskole.

A visit was paid to Czechoslovakia, where at Prague a Conference of the International Protestant League was held. In this the Secretary was accompanied by the Rev. E. J. T. Bagnall, on behalf of the British Organisation.

Thus as the years have passed, the Secretary, acting from the centre, has carried out to distant lands the threads of spiritual intercourse which weave the fabric of the fellowship of the Alliance. This sacred work has been facilitated during Mr. Gooch's secretariat by the presence at the centre, for thirty-four of the forty-two years, of Mr. H. W. Hall, now the able and faithful Assistant-Secretary, and by the good work of lady clerks of equal loyalty and devotion.

CHAPTER XVIII

ALLIANCE LEADERS AND HELPERS

IT is impossible even to name all the eminent men who during the century have taken part in the fellowship and work of the Alliance – they are legion – but it is desirable to mention some representatives that the reader may know the kind of people who constitute this Alliance, generation by generation.

First, there is Sir Culling Eardley, the tactful and gracious Chairman of the Conference of 1846. He was descended from a French Protestant refugee of Queen Elizabeth's time and was deeply interested in the formation of the Alliance, which realised his ideal of the true Church as a world-wide fellowship of believers. He was the first President of the Alliance (British Organisation) and held this position until his death in 1863.

Then there was John Henderson, of Park, Glasgow, a wealthy merchant who, more than any other, may be regarded as the originator of the Alliance. The idea of it arose in his mind, he imparted it to other Christian leaders, and with them took measures to realise it. After the founding of the Alliance he supported it with princely generosity and promoted its character and influence by his own deep piety. He died in 1867. The third person in the central group of founders was Edward Steane, Baptist minister of Denmark Place, Camberwell. Dr. Steane was present at the Liverpool Conference of 1845, and was appointed one of the Secretaries to prepare for the founding Conference. He evidently had the lion's share in shaping the constitution of the Alliance and a chief part in its early administration. He was the first editor of *Evangelical Christendom* and was prominent in European Conferences and in deputations to foreign rulers on behalf of religious liberty. He died in 1882.

In the archives of the Alliance there is preserved a precious volume containing the facsimile signatures of the members of the founding Conference. As one scans the hundreds of names one realises that among them are many that are household words to us after a hundred years.

ALLIANCE LEADERS AND HELPERS

There was Edward Bickersteth, the saintly Rector of Watton, Herts, whose utterances seem always to have breathed the spirit of grace and love.

John Angell James, the Congregational minister of Carr's Lane, Birmingham, a man of evangelical fervour and power, who had been the medium of communication with the transatlantic brethren.

Thomas Binney, the Congregational minister of the Weigh House Chapel, London, a leader of British Nonconformity.

James Hamilton, the popular minister of Regent Square Presbyterian Church, London, for some years editor of *Evangelical Christendom*.

David King, of Glasgow, the minister of John Henderson (of Park), belonging to the United Secession Church of Scotland.

J. S. Blackwood, minister of the Church of Ireland, keenly interested in religious liberty, who went to Constantinople to interview the Grand Vizier of Turkey and obtained the issue of a firman giving religious freedom to all the Sultan's subjects.

J. W. Massie, Manchester, Independent. The writer of *The Evangelical Alliance: its Origin and Development*.

The Hon. and Rev. Baptist W. Noel, Chaplain to Queen Victoria, Minister of St. John's, London, who later joined the Baptist denomination.

T. Byrth, Rector of Wallasey, a distinguished scholar.

R. C. L. Bevan, the first Treasurer of the Alliance, holding that post till 1890.

W. Arthur, Wesleyan minister, author of *The Tongue of Fire*, member of the Alliance nearly fifty years.

Norman McLeod, of Dalkeith; a leader in the Church of Scotland.

John Howard Hinton, London; Baptist minister.

J. Leifchild, London; Independent minister.

The Hon. Arthur Kinnaird, London; Church of England; a stalwart Evangelical.

Lord Roden, Ireland; active in cause of religious liberty.

F. A. Cox, Hackney; Baptist minister.

Newman Hall, Hull; later London; Countess of Huntingdon minister.

Samuel Morley; prominent Congregational layman.

All the above belonged to Great Britain and Ireland, but there was a very large number of founders from other lands.

The most numerous group of these hailed from North America including:

S. H. Cox, Brooklyn; Presbyterian; Dr. Cox showed himself an able and ready debater, taking a frequent part in the inaugural Conference.

W. Patton, New York; Presbyterian; one of the earliest friends of the Alliance movement.

Lyman Beecher, Cincinnati, Ohio; a pastor of seventy years' experience, held in much honour.

S. S. Schmucker, Gettysburg; Lutheran theological tutor; made personal sacrifices in opposition to slavery.

M. M. Clark, Washington; African Methodist Episcopal Church; the negro pastor who created so favourable an impression in the inaugural Conference.

And among the Canadian delegates was:

Richard Hutchinson, Waterloo; Minister of The Advent Church.

From the European Continent came another large contingent of whom a few representatives may be mentioned:

Prof. T. Laharpe, Theological School of Geneva. A ready speaker in English; connected with the Evangelical Society of Geneva, and familiar with the religious conditions of French-speaking Switzerland.

Adolphe Monod, Professor, Montauban University, France. An agreeable representative of French Protestantism, recalling the character and sufferings of the Huguenots.

C. Baup, Vevey (Switzerland). Evangelical Free Church of the Canton de Vaud. The presence of M. Baup was specially touching as he represented the Church in Switzerland which was at that time going through persecution.

J. G. Oncken, Hamburg. The Baptist pioneer of Northern and Eastern Europe; had been fined and imprisoned but went on preaching the Gospel not only in Germany but in Poland, Russia and other countries.

W. Marriott, Basle. In the book of signatures gives his Church as "Evangelical Alliance".

W. Hoffman, President of the Basle Missionary Institution, and Director of Missions connected with it.

E. Kuntze, Pastor of the United Protestant Church in Berlin, an active worker for the Alliance in Germany.

F.A. Tholuck, Halle University (Germany). "A distinguished ornament of German Evangelical Theology".

HONOURABLE WOMEN

The founders of the Alliance appear to have all been of the male sex, but by 1850 it was realised that many ladies had joined its fellowship, and the Council of the British Organisation resolved that measures should be adopted for the formation of Women's Committees in London and all the large towns included in the Organisation, that these might promote the cause by arranging meetings for Christian intercourse, by securing new members and by helping in finance.

From that day to this, Christian women have been among the most loyal and faithful helpers of the Alliance. Many, remembering the act of Mary of Bethany, have sought through the Alliance to bring to the Lord Jesus the anointing of their love.

LEADERS OF FOLLOWING YEARS

As years passed, many other leaders followed in the steps of the founders. One of those best known to the world was Charles Haddon Spurgeon, the great preacher of the Metropolitan (Baptist) Tabernacle, London. Spurgeon came to London in 1854, when in his twentieth year, and with his fervid, evangelical preaching at once attracted crowds. While still in his early ministry be joined the Evangelical Alliance, rejoicing in its witness to Christ and His Cross, but in 1864 he preached sermons against "Baptismal Regeneration" which grieved many members of the Alliance and evoked severe criticisms from them. Spurgeon in consequence withdrew from the Alliance. Towards the end of his life, however, he was deeply troubled by what he felt to be departures from the faith and turned again to the Alliance, rejoining its fellowship. From this time onward he gave the Alliance his warm support, finding in it a bulwark against false teaching. He died in 1892, leaving a church of more than 5,000 members, a college, an orphanage, and twenty-two mission stations. All had come about through the preaching of the Gospel for which the Evangelical Alliance stands.

Among the leaders and helpers of the Alliance there have been some of the class of which St. Paul was thinking when he said that "not many noble" were called.

In addition to those already named, there have been, for example:

Lord Polwarth, who was a member of the Alliance Council fifty-six years, and President of the British Organisation forty-two years, rendering great service to the cause.

Lord Radstock, for more than half a century occupying a leading place among Evangelical Christians, preaching as an evangelist not only in Great Britain but in France, Russia and other lands. He joined the Alliance Council in 1865 and maintained his interest in it till his death in 1913.

Lord Kinnaird, for many years a leader in the Evangelical Alliance, taking the chair at great meetings in Queen's Hall for united prayer, or witness to truth. An athlete in early life, he was a sportsman to the end, using his influence to prevent Sunday games. He died in 1923.

Lord Brentford, earlier known as Sir William Joynson-Hicks, a warm friend of the Alliance, presiding at many of its meetings. A Vice-President of the Alliance till called hence in 1932.

Lord Caldecote, formerly Sir Thomas Inskip, a Vice-President of the Alliance, of which he has long been a valued counsellor, rendering many services, including a visit to Malta to investigate conditions there affecting religious liberty. He is happily with us still.

Lord Bennett, the former Prime Minister of Canada, now residing in England. Deeply interested in Evangelical principles, presides at Alliance gatherings.

In Germany, Count Bernstorff was for many years President of the German branches of the Alliance, and a welcome speaker at its international Conferences. He would advocate the Alliance cause in all circles; a letter to his mother contains the following passage: "You will be impatient to hear something about my interview with Her Majesty. She kept me with her for forty minutes. . . . She questioned me about the Evangelical Alliance, and discussed with me what one might do to rouse interest in it." In the same letter he tells of the Alliance Conference in Dublin and adds: "It seemed like a foretaste of Heaven."

In the United States the Hon. W. E. Dodge rendered distinguished service as President of the American branch of the Alliance: in this capacity he occupied the chair at the great New York Conference of 1873.

ALLIANCE LEADERS AND HELPERS 141

In Sweden, Prince Bernadotte, brother of the King of Sweden, is an ardent supporter of the Evangelical Alliance. For years he has been President of the Swedish branch and when the Scandinavian branch was formed, linking Sweden, Norway and Denmark, the Prince was chosen as its first President. He engages in the general work of the Alliance and entertained at his home our General Secretary when the latter was visiting Sweden for the Alliance.

Among Church leaders it is difficult to choose, but one may mention a few representative names: the Alliance will always honour the memory of Bishop E. H. Bickersteth, of Exeter. He is the son of Edward Bickersteth, one of the founders, and is well-known as author of the hymn "Peace, perfect peace". He long promoted the cause of the Alliance in his diocese and elsewhere.

Bishop E. A. Knox, formerly of Manchester, was also a beloved leader in the Alliance circle. When the revision of the Prayer Book was under consideration he took an active part in opposition, believing that the changes proposed were contrary to the Evangelical character of the Church of England. An address expressing the gratitude of the Alliance for his many services to it was presented to the Bishop in 1930.

Bishop Taylor Smith, Chaplain-General to the Forces for many years, was a Vice-President of the Alliance and a man greatly beloved. Whether in an English parish church, among the natives of Sierra Leone, or with a regiment of soldiers, he was always seeking to win people to Christ. In his later years he gave much help to the Alliance, taking some long journeys with the General Secretary to visit Continental centres. He died and was buried at sea in 1938.

Canon Hay Aitken has been called "the last great Victorian Evangelist". Few men conducted more missions or won more decisions for Christ. He was a man aglow with Evangelical passion, in true accord with the Alliance, to which he belonged. He died in 1927.

Canon Fleming, a distinguished clergyman of West London, was an Hon. Secretary of the Alliance. Both in counsel and in public speech he rendered valued service to the cause.

David MacEwan, Presbyterian minister of Clapham, was one of the earlier Hon. Secretaries to the Alliance. Cherishing memories of the pioneers, many of whom he had known, he would appeal to the later generation to be worthy of the traditions they had left. He died in 1910, at the age of eighty.

F. W. Baedeker was long an honoured member of the Alliance. He was a man of apostolic spirit, travelling to many lands on his Master's business. Especially in Russia he fulfilled his ministry, visiting prisons and leper hospitals, and journeying down the Volga to disseminate the Sacred Word.

Dean Wace, a firm Evangelical, was a Vice-President of the Alliance, giving an influential testimony to the Inspiration and Authority of the Bible.

R. Saillens, a French Evangelical, has been called "the Spurgeon of France". His work was chiefly done in and around Paris: he wrote *The Soul of France*, sketching the work of Evangelism throughout the nineteenth century. He was a welcome speaker at Alliance gatherings in England.

T. J. Pulvertaft, an Irish clergyman, was a member of the Alliance Council and Secretary of the Spanish and Portuguese Church Aid Society. His articles on Spain and Portugal and "Notes" in *Evangelical Christendom* were invaluable.

T. A. Leigh, a Liverpool layman, was a member of the Alliance sixty years, and a generous supporter of the work at home and abroad.

Prebendary Webb-Peploe, a West London clergyman, was an Hon. Secretary of the Alliance. Wise in counsel and eloquent in speech.

Sadhu Sundar Singh, the remarkable Indian Christian, speaking for the Alliance at one of its annual gatherings in London, said: "People who are one in Him" (Christ) "will have that Christian love which the World's Evangelical Alliance represents." In his Eastern robe and with his calm, gracious countenance, Sundar Singh seemed to many as like their idea of Christ, and certainly in his spirit there was much of the likeness of Christ. In the course of his missionary wanderings he visited Tibet and has not been heard of since. No doubt he passed from those bleak mountains to the land of glory.

Sir Donald Maclean was a Vice-President of the Alliance and one who, while occupying a great position in the political life of the nation, was always a humble servant of Christ. Towards the end of his life he said: "After a long experience in public life, there is nothing which comes up to, or ever

ALLIANCE LEADERS AND HELPERS

will approach in vital importance, the regeneration of the individual soul through the merits of our Lord Jesus Christ."

F. B. Meyer, one of the most beloved and honoured men of modern times, was for many years a member of the Alliance Council. He first came into contact with the Alliance as a young minister, the assistant of C. M. Birrell, of Liverpool. After that, throughout his life he entered into the work and witness of the Alliance.

W. Fuller Gooch, the father of the General Secretary of the Alliance, was himself an honoured member of its Council. He fulfilled fruitful ministries in Norfolk, Cornwall and London, always loyal to the Evangel and cherishing the spirit of loving unity with God's people of whatever name.

W. Y. Fullerton, a great-souled Irishman, as pastor, evangelist and missionary organiser equally eminent, was for years a member of the Alliance Council and a familiar speaker on its platforms. Alliance listeners will remember the glow with which he would quote, from the French version of a psalm, the words: "It is He that delivers magnificently." He will be immortalised by his hymn, "The Saviour of the World".

Carey Bonner, Baptist minister and Sunday School leader, was a member of the Alliance Council and a valued sharer in its work. With literary and musical gifts he would prepare a cantata for an Alliance demonstration and then conduct a great choir in Queen's Hall, or the Albert Hall, in rendering it.

Dinsdale T. Young, the great Methodist preacher, was for more than thirty years a member of the Council of the Alliance. A man of firm convictions and gracious sympathies, he drew great congregations to the Central Hall, Westminster, and always uplifted Christ and His Cross to them. A little before the end of his life he spoke for the Alliance at the Mansion House on "The Magnificent Gospel".

G. Campbell Morgan was a Vice-President of the Alliance and a warm friend of its work. His messages at its gatherings were always inspiring. His ministry, exercised partly in the United States and partly in England, tended to draw the two nations together, and still more to promote the unity of Christians. He was essentially a Bible teacher.

Among those who have recently passed away there are some who rendered special service to the Alliance.

Sir Andrew Wingate, a devoted friend of the Alliance, fostered its interests over a long period of years, acting for some time as Chairman of the Executive Council.

R. C. Gillie, the gifted Presbyterian minister, was for years an Hon. Secretary of the Alliance. An able administrator and a speaker of great charm, he sought to present the Evangelical message in the language of today.

R. C. Hart Dyke was for many years the Treasurer of the British Organisation and the Chairman of the Executive Council. Mr. Hart Dyke's knowledge of business and unfailing tact made him an ideal Chairman, and his intimate acquaintance with Alliance history and his kindly spirit gave point and attractiveness to his public addresses. He and Mrs. Hart Dyke delighted to show hospitality to Alliance representatives in their pleasant Hadley Wood home.

W. Talbot Rice, a West London clergyman, was for many years an Hon. Secretary of the Alliance. In this capacity his courtesy and kindness, joined with businesslike acumen, won him success in the council chamber, while his large-minded loyalty to the Gospel made him an effective speaker on the Alliance platform. Mr. Talbot Rice will not be soon forgotten.

It is invidious to choose persons for mention from the many living helpers of the Alliance, but there are two whose official positions give them special opportunities for service.

One is the Rt. Hon. Isaac Foot, the recently-appointed Treasurer of the British Organisation and Chairman of the Executive. Mr. Foot is this year the Lord Mayor of Plymouth. He brings to his Alliance task the fruits of a long municipal and political experience, added to an intimate acquaintance with Church history, especially of the Reformation and Puritan periods. With all this is linked warm Evangelical conviction.

The other friend is the Rev. J. Chalmers Lyon, Presbyterian minister of Hampstead, who is the present Free Church Hon. Secretary of the Alliance. Mr. Lyon has given many years of devoted service to the Alliance. Besides attending its Councils, and often presiding at them, he takes a prominent part in its public gatherings and has joined the General Secretary in several of his Continental journeys, notably to Spain and Portugal, to Germany and Poland. He is a man of warm heart and ready speech, who wins his audience and so makes a way for the entrance of his message. He has also a facility in verse, seen in the pages of *Evangelical Christendom*.

I have thus sought to introduce, with brief touches of characterisation, representatives of the men who have made Alliance history during a hundred years. They are of many Churches, many races, many casts of mind, yet they are deeply one, because united in their faith in Christ and their loyalty to the Gospel.

Where can you find a succession of greater men, held together through a century by a spiritual consensus?

Their secret is in the Alliance motto:

Unum Corpus Sumus In Christo.

CHAPTER XIX

WHAT OF THE FUTURE?

OUR review has shown that the World's Evangelical Alliance has been enabled by God to accomplish great things during its century of history. It came into being at a time of religious depression and brought with it a quickening of spiritual life. It created a new fellowship among Christians of many denominations and gave the Christian Church a new unity.

Especially was the Alliance welcomed on the Continent by bands of believers who had felt themselves lonely and hard-pressed, and now found themselves part of a great family with resources hitherto unknown. The result was seen in the series of great international Conferences in the first half-century. These made possible united action for Evangelism, the relief of persecuted Christians, and opposition to social evils, Sabbath desecration and infidelity.

The second half-century has seen a concentration of strength within the various nations, expressing itself in a growing initiative. In London, for example, the birthplace of the Alliance, there has been an extraordinary series of demonstrations in the largest halls available, expressing Christian principles and giving guidance which has certainly been of influence in the community. In the promotion of prayer the Alliance has exercised leadership, not only in the nation in time of war, but throughout the world in the opening days of each new year.

Now the questions arise, Can the Alliance continue its usefulness? and Is it likely to be needed under the changed conditions of this new time? That the conditions are changed admits of no doubt. A hundred years ago the Alliance stood alone as a uniting Christian fellowship. Since that time many other uniting movements have sprung up. Early in the Alliance century, came the Y.M.C.A. and the Y.W.C.A., and later the Student Christian Movement, linking young people of various Churches for mutual help; half-way down the century came the Free Church Council, later the Free Church Federal Council, bringing together the Churches of Nonconformity;

and recently the British Council, now the World Council, of Churches.

With all these, there is still a place for the Evangelical Alliance. These unions bring together many shades of belief, but there is yet need of one which stands for the spiritual unity of all with whom the Cross of Christ is central whether Anglicans or Free Churchmen, young or old.

The question of reunion among the Churches is still unsettled. Some are striving for organic union, but others feel that this is not possible without disloyalty to convictions which Churches hold sacred, Any unity which infringed principle would be loss and not gain. Here the value of the Evangelical Alliance comes in; it is a voluntary fellowship of Christians of every Church who are one in the central truths of the Evangelical faith. Its members have their own denominational affinities, but agree on the deeper principles of the Christian Revelation. "Holding the Head", they realise their unity with the other members of the Body of Christ.

The Evangelical Alliance may be regarded as the advance guard of the Christian army. It exists to promote the proclamation of the Gospel which is the God-given instrument for the salvation of men. It presents the message of the love that redeems to a race in which all have sinned. And this message is just as essential to-day as a hundred years ago.

Indeed the facts of our time accentuate the need for it. We are all conscious of the changed situation in religion. The falling off in attendance at places of worship is a cause of widespread distress. It is estimated that only ten per cent of the population of England regularly attends Church; another ten per cent is opposed to religion, and the remainder are either indifferent or nominally interested. For the majority the Churches might cease to exist without any real difference coming into their life.

The causes of this state of things are various. Probably the chief is the loss of the basic belief in the facts on which religion rests. How has this loss of belief come about? No doubt, through neglect of the Bible, and this has been largely caused by the influence of the humanistic philosophy which has made men cease to look beyond man. God has not been in their thoughts and His word has not been consulted.

With the eternal realm shut out from view, the temporal

scene has been absorbing. The discoveries of science – aeroplane, submarine, wireless – and the political and military events of the latest years have absorbed attention. The disappearance for multitudes of the divine standards has brought the inevitable casting off of restraint. Pleasure and gain are eagerly sought and crime abounds.

And now the gravity of the hour is deepened by the menace of the atomic bomb. It is a time when life and death are in the balance. Human statecraft has failed us and the race is in danger. It is time for all who know the Way of Life to be up and doing. To the Evangelical Alliance comes the trumpet-call of a new and great opportunity.

Other facts of the day emphasise the need of the Alliance. All through its history the Alliance has stood for religious liberty. That cause is not yet fully won in many lands to-day. In not a few the freedom of the spirit is denied. Totalitarian Governments claim the right to dominate soul as well as body. Wherever the Church of Rome has sway, in South America, Spain, Malta, or elsewhere, the people are held down by the iron hand of the priest. And even in Great Britain, where the cause of the Reformation triumphed 400 years ago, Rome seeks in subtle ways to regain her hold upon us. The warnings of the Alliance against Roman error are still called for, and her action for religious liberty is as necessary as when she roused Europe to secure the release of Matamoros and the Madiai.

But is the Alliance able to-day to meet the need that calls her? She is, if love and prayer and the Gospel are still living realities. These are interwoven with her being. But the Alliance needs continual renewal by the incoming of new lives into her own. She has no existence apart from the people of God.

There is today a special call to the young people who love Christ to come forward in this holy cause. Young men and young women from the Universities and Colleges, and those who have influence in industrial circles, are needed to take the places once held by leaders now with God. The tide of education rises everywhere, and to reach the new generation knowledge of the thought and life of the day is essential. Every power needs to be laid on the altar for Christ.

Much stress is laid to-day on the social aspects of the Gospel. The Evangelical Alliance is not unmindful of these.

She has always put first the regeneration of the soul, but she has also given herself to care for the body. She threw herself into the anti-slavery crusade and was in deep sympathy with Lord Shaftesbury and Florence Nightingale, with Muller and Spurgeon, with Barnardo and Quarrier.

There are social crusades yet to be waged and the Alliance will take her part in them, knowing that the Gospel of the Cross is the great instrument for the casting down of abuses and the building up of the Kingdom of Righteousness. The Alliance has given unvarying support to the missionary movement and the results of this are seen in the Southern Seas, where erstwhile headhunters and cannibals are now Christians, and in the Congo, where cruelty and superstition have given place to the light and joy and freedom of the children of God. It is Jesus who builds the new world.

The victories of the last century now present a new challenge. The "Younger" Churches, recently brought to Christ, whose representatives formed the majority at the great Missionary Conference at Tambaram, now open up new areas to Christian influence. They themselves need fellowship with the older Churches of the world and their "hinterlands" present fresh spheres for Evangelism.

In thinking of the preaching of the Gospel in new lands one cannot forget our Saviour's declaration that when the Gospel has been preached in all the world for a witness to all nations, "then shall the end come". So the fulfilment of the task of the Alliance and its co-workers will be a preparation for the great day when our Lord will come in His Glory.

The future may require new methods of Evangelism. The "Commando" is proving successful in reaching working people in their factories with speech and song and friendly understanding: the youth clubs are proving valuable in drawing and holding young people within the circle of the Church's interests; the Press is probably capable of being used more fully in public appeal. The help of the laity, as in the past, will be invaluable in the daily contacts of the home, of business, or of travel.

But, whatever new methods may be adopted in the future, the World's Evangelical Alliance will still rely on the great primal facts – the presence with His people of the Lord Jesus in living and inspiring fellowship; the appeal of the infinite love of God supremely manifested at Calvary; and the power of the Holy Spirit to equip the worker and convict, convert and sanctify the hearer.

The Church of Christ needs a more radiant and joyous experience, the result of a deepening communion with God and a more ready obedience to His Will. When this is hers, history shows that God through her will reach and bless the people around her, as He did in the great revivals of Pentecost, of the eighteenth century, of 1859, and of 1905.

We are not left to a vague hope in this matter. We have a Word upon which to rest. One is reminded of the great answer given by Judson, the missionary to Burma, when he was asked what he thought of the future, and in spite of all difficulties he said, "The future is bright as the promises of God". There are problems in the future for the Evangelical Alliance and for the whole Church of God, but we have promises too – "They that wait upon the Lord shall renew their strength". "Ye shall receive power after that the Holy Ghost is come upon you." "I, if I be lifted up from the earth, will draw all men unto me."

There is the assurance of the future of the World's Evangelical Alliance.

EPILOGUE

WHAT THE FUTURE DID HOLD?

IN his last chapter above, Dr Ewing reminded his readers that in 1846 *"the Alliance stood alone as a uniting Christian fellowship"* since when many other uniting movements had sprung up which brought together *"many shades of belief, but there is yet need of one which stands for the spiritual unity of all with whom the Cross of Christ is central"*. He goes on to say that *"some are striving for organic union, but others feel that this is not possible without disloyalty to convictions which Churches hold sacred"* and he asserted the value of the Evangelical Alliance as a voluntary fellowship of Christians of every Church who are one in the central truths of the Evangelical faith. Those central truths were regarded as "fundamental" to the Christian faith as proclaimed by the Apostles and as recorded in Scripture.

From the 1920's onwards those who had moved on from a commitment to the fundamental doctrines of the historic Christian faith increasingly disparaged those who remained committed to Scripture, referring to them as "fundamentalists". Even today (January 2022) the website of the World Council of Churches states unambiguously *"a first Evangelical Alliance was formed as early as 1846; it ceased to function after World War I, i.e. in the period marked by the rise of fundamentalism"*. Readers will make their own minds up as to how in 1946 Dr Ewing was able to write in the history of the WEA up to that date ending with a chapter "What of the future?" if it has ceased to function after the First World War.

The future was very uncertain. The Second World War had ravaged the church on the continent of Europe. Across the Atlantic in 1942 during the darkest period of the war American evangelicals set up the National Association of Evangelicals. When hostilities ceased in 1945 they sought to rebuild the shattered evangelical relationships with their own equivalent of a "Marshall Plan". This resulted in the re-establishment of Alliance work as the "World Evangelical Fellowship" at a re-founding conference in the Netherlands in 1951. The reason for the change of name was that the word "Alliance" retained many connotations of military alliances between nations during the conflict.

The UK Evangelical Alliance worked with the Americans in helping to revive evangelical the work across the world. Most alliances on the European continent were reluctant to join the revised alliance headed by "American fundamentalists" and did not do so. They continued with the old arrangements (even though they had ceased to exist in 1918!) and held and annual conference of the regional body, the European Evangelical Alliance. When I joined the staff of the WEF in 1969 I attended their annual conferences but was less than impressed with the lack of evangelical commitment. It was a largely "Protestant" (in the German language "Evangelische") body which Bible believing Christians did not wish to join. Incidentally, from 1974 onwards the Lausanne Committee filled this void on the continent. That year I attended my last old-style EEA annual conference. I resolved not to waste my time by attending another EEA conference until the whole of their generation had died out – rather like God's decision regarding the Israelites in the Wilderness for 40 years! I had attended the 1974 Lausanne Congress. That was the sort of evangelicalism we needed.

That generation did die out. In the 1980s Gordon Showell-Rogers, from the EA staff in London, was appointed as EEA General Secretary and did a sterling work with the Continental alliances in bringing them back a commitment to the fundamentals of the historic Christian faith and becoming members of the WEF. Since that time the WEA has grown from a constituency of 100,000,000 to 625,000,000 evangelical Christians across the world who, in Dr Ewing's words stand *"for the spiritual unity of all with whom the Cross of Christ is central"*, while the ecumenical organisations have steadily declined.

Like him, we cannot foretell the future but if we remain faithful to the fundamental truths of the Christian faith we can be assured that on the biblical rock of scripture God will continue to build His church and the gates of hell will not prevail against it.

JOHN LANGLOIS

WEA International Council Member

January 2022

INDEX

A

Achilli, Dr., 59, 60
Adeney, J. H., 104
African International League, 95
Aitken, Canon Hay, 141
Alexander, General, 30, 68
Alexander II, Tsar of Russia, 70
Alfonso, King of Spain, 76
Alford, Dean, 28
Alhama, Senor, 66
Alliance, The Evangelical, 17
Ambedkar, Dr., 104
Amsterdam Conference, 29
Anderson, Sir Robert, 87
Angus, Joseph, 35
Armenia, 73
Arnold, A. I., 32, 35, 132
Arthur, W., 29, 98, 137
Ashley, Lord, 81
Aubrey, M. E., 116
Augsburg Confession, 56

B

Baedeker, F. W., 42, 114, 142
Bagnall, E. J. T., 113, 135
Bahaism, 90, 91
Baird, R., 120, 121
Baldwin, Lord, 112
Balmer, Dr., 13
Baptist Missionary Society, 102
Barber, W. T. A., 109
Barker, Ernest, 116
Barnardo, T. J., 149
Barrett, G. S., 107
Barrows, Major-General, 132
Basis, The Doctrinal, 17, 129
Basle Conference, 31
Baup, C., 20, 138
Beecher, Henry Ward, 31
Beecher, Lyman, 138
Bennett, Lord, 140
Berlin Conference, 27
Berlin International Council, 95
Bernadotte, Prince, 134, 141
Bernstorff, Count, 30, 140
Berry, S. M., 116

Besant, Mrs. Annie, 88, 91
Bevan, F. A., 107, 130
Bevan, R. C. L., 137
Bevan, W., 132
Bickersteth, E., 15, 17 21 41 80 120, 132, 137
Bickersteth, E. H., 25, 34, 35, 141
Binney, T., 15, 137
Birdwood, Sir W., 112
Birks, T. R., 29, 117
Birrell, C. M., 143
Bismarck, Prince, 132
Blackwood, J. S., 15, 137
Blavatsky, Madame, 88
Bledisloe, Lord, 113
Bonar, Horatius, 127
Bonner, Carey, 112, 143
Bonnet, L., 22
Boxer Riots, 124
Bradley, Dean, 35
Brazil, 77
Brentford, Lord, 140
Bright, John, 11
British Empire Bungalow, 47
British and Foreign Bible society,
Brown, Allan, 116
Brown, Dame Edith, 104
Buchanan, R., IS, 16
Bunting, W. M., 15, 117, 132
Bunyan, John, 111, 112
Bursche, Bishop, 135
Byrth, T., 137

C

Cabrera, Don Fernando, 45, 110, 111
Cairns, Principal, 33
Caldecote, Lord, 140
Calvin, John, 29
Campbell, Dr., 15
Campbell, J. H., M.P., 54
Canada, 23
Candlish, Dr., 13, 15
Canterbury, Archbishop of, 39, 81, 86, 126
Canton de Vaud, 58
Carey, William, 12, 32

153

Cash, Bishop Wilson, 104
Catholic Action, 57
Central America, 103
Ceylon Convert, 100
Chalmers, Thomas, 11, 13, 19, 118, 119
Chalmers, W., 117
Chatelain, Heli, 94
Cheng Ching, Yi, 38
Chiang Kai-Shek, Generalissimo, 126
China, 37
Christlieb, Pastor, 107
Clark, M. M., 19, 138
Clifford, John, 54
Cobden, Richard, 11
Comber, Thomas, 101
Compton-Rickett, Sir J., 40
Confessional, The, 52
Consort, Prince, 81
Constantinople, 24, 100
Convents, Inspection of, 52
Cook, Charles, 20
Copenhagen Conference, 32
Corkey, W., 54
Corn Laws, 11
Cox, F. A., 137
Cox, S. H., 15, 138
Crewe, Marquis of, 115
Cumming, J., 98

D
Danzig, Archdeacon of, 13
Darwin, Charles, 12
D'Aubigne, C. Merle, 37, 110
D'Aubigne J.H. Merle 13, 15, 119
Davidson, Archbishop, 39
Davis, J., 132
Denmark, H. M. King of, 32
De Tocqueville, M., 60
Disraeli, Benjamin, 11
Disruption, The, 11
Dobson, J. P., 132
Dodge, Hon. W.E., 30, 140
Dollinger, Dr., 51
Dublin, 35
Duff, Alexander, 12, 99

E
Eardley, Sir Culling, Bart., 15, 16, 17, 59, 64, 81, 98, 131, 136
Ebury, Lord, 71
Eddy, Mrs., 89

Egypt, 72
English Bible, 116
Erasmus, 31
Estonia, 43, 134
Evangelisation, Manifesto on, 48
Ewing, J. W., 113, 131

F
Factory Act, 11
Fernendez, Pablo, 75
Field, E. P., 132
Field, General Sir John, 132
Fisch, Georges, 28
Fleming, Canon, 141
Florence, 33, 95
Foot, Rt. Hon. Isaac, 114, 115, 131, 144
Foxe, John, 115
France, 22
Francis Joseph I, Emperor of Austria, 72
Frederick II, King of Prussia, 28
Frederick William IV, King of Prussia, 27, 28, 63, 64
Freemasons' Hall, 15, 25, 29
Fullerton, W. Y., 109, I 10, I 11, 125, 143

G
Garibaldi, 29
Geneva, 28, 29, 82
George V, King, and Queen Mary, 108, 112
George VI, King, and Queen Elizabeth, 115, 131
Germany, 22
Geymonat, Dr., 33, 61
Gibbon, Edward, 28
Gillie, R. C., 83, I 08, 113, 130, 144
Girdlestone, Canon, 90
Gladstone, William Ewart, 11, 52
Glass, F.C., 77
Gold Coast, 37
Gooch, H. Martyn, 56, 57, 114, 115, 125, 128, 131, 133-135
Gooch, W. Fuller, 0, 108, 143
Gordon, General, C.G., 95
Gortschakoff, Prince, 70
Grandpierre, Dr., 26
Grant, President, U.S.A., 30
Granville, Lord, 71
Greece, 47

Green, J.E., 116
Grenfell, G., 101
Grubb, K., 103
Guatemala, 103
Guicciardini, Count, 61
Guthrie, T., 30

H

Haddo, Lord, 83
Hall, Newman, 35, 137
Hamaradka, Professor, 110
Hamilton, General Sir Ian, 115
Hamilton, James, 14, 26, 80, 132, 137
Hanson, G., 90, 111
Harris, J., 117
Hart-Dyke R. C., 109, 110, 130, 144
Hanzell, Bishop, 107
Hasse, Bishop, 87
Havelock, Sir Henry, 123
Hayes, President, U.S.A., 83
Heim, Karl, 114
Helenius, Pastor, 110
Henderson, John, 13, 15, 80, 136
Hill, Rowland, 123
Hinton, J. H., 137
Hitler, 87
Hoffman, W., 138
Holy Cross, Society of, 52
Hongkong, 99
Hooper, Bishop, 31
Hoyois, Pastor, 110
Humbert, King of Italy, 34
Hus, John, 53
Hutchinson, R., 138

I

India, 23
Immaculate Conception, Dogma, 50
"Infallibility" of the Pope, 51
Inskip, Sir Thomas, 109, 115, 116
Isabella II, Queen of Spain, 68
Italy, 77

J

Jackson, C., 132
Jackson, H.R.T., 132
James, John Angell, 13, 14, 15, 60, 80, 137
Janni, Pastor, 110, 111
Japan, 71, 77

Jones, J. D., 109
Joynson-Hicks, Sir William, 109, 110, 111

K

Kant, Immanuel, 86
Kayayan, Professor, 73
Kent, Duke of, 112, 115
Kilburn, J. D., 42
King, David, 13, 26, 137
Kinnaird, Hon. Arthur, 15, 67, 137
Kinnaird, Lord, 40, 54, 107, 108, 130, 140
Kitching, Archdeacon, 104, 105
Knox, Bishop, E. A., 141
Korea, 107
Krummacher, Dr., 28
Kuntze, E., 22, 138

L

Laborde, Abbe, 50
Labrador, Juan, 76
Laharpe, T., 138
Lamont, Dr .• 115
Lang, Archbishop, 111
Langston, E. L., 89, 1 35
La Salette, The "Miracle" of, 50
Latimer, Hugh, 111
Lees, Harrington C., 90
Leifchild, J., 15, 132, 137
Leigh, T. and Mrs. Leigh, 110, 142
Lester, J. W., 132
Lewis, H. Elvet, 11O
Liddell, Eric, 125
Liverpool, Conference, 14, 35
Livingstone, David, 12, 94, 1OI
Loja, Insurrection at, 66
London, 25, 29, 34, 36
London, Bishop of, 115
London County Council, 83
London Missionary Society, 70, 98, 101
London, Recorder of, 38
Los von Rom, 53
Ludhiana, 36, 100, 104
Luther, Martin, 108
Lyon, J. Chalmers, 114, 126, 134, 144

M

Macewan, David, 141

Macgregor, D. C., 109
Maclean, Sir Donald, 109, 142
Madagascar, 70
Madden, Archdeacon, 111
Madiai, The, 61, 62, 63
Madrid, 45
Malan, Cesar, 86
Malines, Conversations at, 55
Malta, 45, 76
Marriott, W., 138
Marsovan, 73
Martin, F., 20
Massie, J. w., 15, 120, 137
Matamoros, Manuel, 65-69
McArthur, Sir W., 32
McCheyne, R.M., 119
McCrie, T., 29
McLeod, Norman, 137
McNeill, John, 47, 110
Melson, Dr., 60
Methodism, American, 31
Meyer, F. B., 114, 143
Mildmay, Conference, 35
"Milk-eaters", 121
Moffat, Robert, 12, 101
Monod, Adolphe, 15, 20, 138
Monod, E., 82 Monod, G., 28
Montpensier, Duc de, 68
Moody, D. L., 41
Moreira, E., 46
Moreton, R. H., 46
Morgan, G. Campbell, 115, 143
Morley, Samuel, 137
Moscow, 43
Mott, J. R., 105
Moule, Bishop Handley, 107
Millier, G., 149

N

Nagel, Herr, 110, 111
Naville, E., 82
Nations, League of, 109
Nestorian Christians, 69
"Ne Temere" Decree, 53, 54
Newman, J. H., 12, 120
New York, Conference, 30
Nicolai, Baron, 107
Nietzsche, 87
Nightingale, Florence, 149
Nightindale, Thomas, 110
Nilsson, Frederick, 60

Noel, Hon. Baptist W. Noel, 14, 15, 28, 29, 59, 137
Norwich, Bishop Pollock, of, 112, I 13, 115, 116
Nyasaland, 37

O

Oecolampadius, 31
Old Catholic Church, 52
Oncke, J. G., 85, 138
Oporto, 74
Oroomiah, 69
Orr, James, 90
Osborn, John, 15

P

Padin, Carmen, 76, 77
Palmerston, Lord, 60, 67, 81, 82
Paris, 26, 37, 82
Paris and Lyons Railway, 82
Parker, Joseph, 31
Parkes, Sir Harry, 71
Paterson, Sinclair, 86
Paton, J. G., 124
Patton, W., 13, 15, 28, 138
"Pearl of Days", 81
Peel, Sir Robert, 11, 66, 67,
Pennefather, W., 35
Persia, 69
Peru, 75
Petrie, Sir Flinders, I 26
Pobedonostzeff, M., 72, 73
Podin, Adam, 42-44, 110, 134
Poland, 44
Polwarth, Lord, 34, 140
Portugal, 24, 46, 74
Portugal, King of, 74
Prayer Book, Revision of, 55, 56
Prayer, Universal Week of, 36, 100, 106
Pressense, Dr. de, 67, 85
Protestant League, 56
Pulvertaft, T. 1., 142

Q

Quarrier, W., 149

R

Radstock, Lord, 140
Ramabai, Pandita, 89, 102
Resolutions, The Practical, 20
Reval, 43
Rice, Hon. W. Talbot, 113, 144

INDEX 157

Richards, J. R., 90
Richey, M., 23 .
Ridley, Nicholas, II I
Roberts, Field-Marshal, Lord, 40
Robertson, W.B., 28
Roden, Lord, 137
Roder, General, 82
Roman, Francisco, 122
Rosebery, Lord, 73
Roskilde, Cathedral, 33
Rousseau, 86
Row, Prebendary C. A., 86
Rumania, 77, I 04
Rumanian Railways, 82
Russell, C. T., 91
Russell, Lord John, 62, 67
Russia, 42, 70, 71, 72

S

Saillens, R., 107, 142
San Francisco Conference, 78
Sankey, Ira, D., 41
Saxe, Meioingen, 63
Saxony, 74
Schmettau, H., 68, 132
Schmid, Professor, 81
Schmucker, S. S., I 38
Science, Hall of, 86
Scottish Church Union, 125
Selbie, W. B., 108
Shaftesbury, The 7th Earl of, 11, 67, 149
Shanghai, JS
Simpson, Carnegie, 108
Sing, Sadhu Sundar, 142
Slavery, The Question of, 18
Smith, Gipsy, 47, 116
Somervell, Howard, 125
Spain, 24, 45, 75, 76, 77, 78
Sparham, C. G., 37
Spurgeon, C. H., 42, 101, 124, 139, 149
St. Paul's Cathedral, 38
Stalin, Generalissimo, 78
Stanford, C., 40
Stamp, Sir Josiah, 116
Stanley, H. M., 95
Steane, E., 15, 29, 41, 60, 117, 132. 136
Stegagna, Dr., 110
Stoddart, Miss Jane T., 88, 103
Stoughton, John, 31, 120

Stuttgart, Conference, 81
Sunday Games in Parks, 83
Sweden, 23

T

Tambaram, Conference, 105, 149
Taylor-Smith, Bishop, 110, I 12, 114, 134, 141
Temple, J. R., 102
Tetuan, Duke of, 68
Theology, the "New", 90
Tholuck, F. A.G., 15, 20, 138
Thomson, James, 121
Thorn, Hospital, 44
Thorpe, A. St. John, 135
Thoumaian, Professor, 73
Thyatira, Archbishop of, 38
Tiberias, 37
"Times", The, 32, 62, 69
Tinling, Miss C., 104
Tractarian, Movement, 12
Tucker, Bishop, 96
Turkey, 24, 64
Turkey, Sultan of, 64, 65
Tuscany, Duke of, 61
Tyndale, William, 114, 115

U

Uganda, Bishop of, 103
Uganda;: the King's letter, 105
Underhill, E. B., 32 30
United States, 19, 23, 30

V

Van Oosterzee, Professor, 30
Victoria, H.M. Queen, 11, 26, 81
Volga, River Mission, 43
Voltaire, 28, 85

W

Wiley, Bishop, 101
Wilkinson, A. H., 131
Williams, John, 12
Williamson, Andrew, 113
Wilson, John, 12
Wilson, President Woodrow, 126
Winslow, Forbes, 88
Wise, A. R., 113
Witness, Week of, 47
Woolley, Sir Leonard, 126
Wylie, J. A., 49
Wace, Dean, 107, 108, 142
Wakefield, Sir C., 108

Waldensian Synod, 133
Wales, Prince of, 113
War Prayer Meetings, 38
Wardlaw, Ralph, 16, 80
Warns, Pastor, 42
Weling, Fraulein Von, 114
Webb-Peploe, Prebendary, 108, 142
Wesley, John, 31, 127
Whately, Archbishop, 14
Whitsuntide calls to Prayer, 39
Wiecbork, "Mother-house", 44
Wilberforce, William, 97, 119

Y

York, Duke and Duchess of, 125, 127
Young, Dinsdale T., 130, 143
Younger, W., 113

Z

Zinzendorf, Count, 127
Zwemer, Dr., 102
Zwigli, Ulrich 134

The glorious company of the apostles:
praise Thee.

The goodly fellowship of the prophets:
praise Thee.

The noble army of martyrs:
praise Thee.

The holy church throughout all the world
doth acknowledge Thee.